No Common Place

The Holocaust Testimony of

Alina Bacall-Zwirn

The
Holocaust
Testimony
of Alina
Bacall-
Zwirn

No Common Place

Alina Bacall-Zwirn

and Jared Stark

University of Nebraska Press

Lincoln and London

© 1999 by the
University of Nebraska Press
All rights reserved
Manufactured in the United States of America

Library of Congress
Cataloging-in-Publication Data
Bacall-Zwirn, Alina, 1922–1997.
No common place : the Holocaust testimony of Alina Bacall-Zwirn /
Alina Bacall-Zwirn and Jared Stark.
   p.   cm.
Includes bibliographical references.
ISBN 0-8032-1296-8 (cl.: alk. paper)
1. Bacall-Zwirn, Alina, 1922–1997—Interviews.   2. Bacall, Leo,
1915–1984.   3. Jews—Poland—Warsaw—Biography.   4. Holocaust,
Jewish (1939–1945)—Poland—Warsaw—Personal narratives.
5. Auschwitz (Concentration camp)   6. Warsaw (Poland)—Biography.
I. Stark, Jared, 1967–   .   II. Title.
DS135.P63A13 1999   99-12593
940.53'18'092   CIP
[b]—DC21

Alina dedicates this book

to Leo and to the members of

both of their families who died

in the Holocaust

CONTENTS

The following pages were composed from interviews, letters, and other documents concerning Alina Bacall-Zwirn, born Alinka Handszer in Warsaw, Poland, on February 5, 1922, and her husband, Leo Bacall, born Leshek Bakalczuk in Davidgrodek, Poland, on July 12, 1915. Leo and Alina were married in the Warsaw ghetto on September 7, 1941. They immigrated together to the United States in 1949 and lived in New York and New Jersey until they retired to Tamarac, Florida, in 1978. Leo died in 1984, and Alina later married Charlie Zwirn. After a yearlong battle with lung cancer, she died, surrounded by her family, on the morning of April 3, 1997, one month after the completion of this manuscript. She is survived by her three children — George, Walter, and Sophia — and six grandchildren, the youngest of whom was born just four months before Alina's death. "The family," Alina told me the last time I saw her, in March 1997, "is finally getting bigger."

I first met Alina in January 1993, at her home in Florida. Alina, together with her daughter, Sophia, who was visiting from Connecticut, talked to me about Leo's frustrated efforts to publish a book about his and his wife's experiences in the Holocaust. A decade before he died he had prepared a manuscript with the assistance of a freelance writer, but due to a perceived lack of an audience for Holocaust narratives, as well as to problems of style and organization within the manuscript itself, the story was never published. Alina and her family wondered whether "One Small Candle" (as the manuscript was titled) could be edited for publication. But Alina realized that, despite growing interest in the testimony of survivors of the Holocaust, the problems of "One Small Candle" could not be solved merely by editing or minor revisions. Not only were there factual errors, but Alina felt that the manuscript ascribed thoughts to Leo and her that were not their own. "He [the writer] put in his philosophy too much," she later told me.

Together we developed an alternative strategy. An immigrant to the United States in 1949, Alina felt too uncomfortable with English to pen her own history. Yet I was hesitant to say in other words, my words, what only she could tell. In a grant application to the Memorial Foundation for Jewish Culture, which generously funded early stages of this work, I described what we decided to do:

> This project will entail the collecting, organizing, and editing of written documents and testimonies in order to convey both the prewar and wartime experiences of Alina and Leo Bacall, as well as their struggle to remember and narrate this history.
>
> Leo Bacall died in 1984, leaving his wife and children with his unfulfilled need to see his story publicly remembered. He left behind fragments of this story—an unedited manuscript, newspaper clippings, letters, photographs. His wife, Alina, was always unwilling to bear recounting her experiences. However, the burden of her husband's memory has motivated her to begin to speak and write about her past.

Although my hand in the current project will be evident to the reader, I have endeavored to avoid "putting in my philosophy" as much as possible. At least, I have not "ghost-written" this history in such a way that my words would be indistinguishable from Alina's. What philosophy there is inheres principally in the method of composition, inspired by the work being done at the Fortunoff Video Archive for Holocaust Testimonies at Yale and at similar projects. The questions I ask, how I organize the material, and my marginal comments will inevitably and necessarily give the reader a sense of my own preoccupations. But these, I hope, do not intrude into Alina's testimony.

Our interviews were conducted over two years—in Florida, in Connecticut, and in Washington DC, where we attended the dedication ceremony of the United States Holocaust Memorial Museum together. Alina also spoke to Dana Kline and Susan Millen, two experienced interviewers at the Fortunoff Video Archive at Yale. Transcripts of these interviews make up the main part of *No Common Place*; mixed in are excerpts from letters and other documents pertaining to Alina's life both during and after the Holocaust. Drafts of transcripts were prepared by Alina's daughter, Sophia, by two independent transcribers, and by me. I have vetted them all for accuracy and whatever errors remain are mine. As anyone who has tried to transcribe an interview can attest, absolute accuracy is an ideal but not a real possibility. The Eastern European heritage audible in Alina's beautiful voice, as well as the vicissitudes of my recording equipment, have led me to listen to each tape numerous times in order to be as accurate as possible. Consonant with the decision to convey Alina's story in Alina's words, I tried to "correct" Alina's speech for grammar and syntax as little as possible. If some readers find it tedious to see the improvisations of a nonnative English speaker consigned to paper, I hope that others will begin not only to sound out Alina's words, but to hear, in the slowed-down language of the written page, how these words articulate an experience that no degree of eloquence could repair.

The form of this book derives both from the *yizker-bikher,* or memorial books, that persecuted Eastern European Jewish communities have created to preserve and commemorate their histories and from the tradition of "commonplace books," collections of quotations, bits of lore, anecdotes, and thoughts. Like a memorial book or a commonplace book, this story is structured as a collection of quotations reflecting different voices, moods, times, and places. But these quotations do not always join fluidly with one another. At times they come into conflict, even contradiction. At times it is unclear who is speaking, and what story is being told. We have to bring a certain degree of openness and patience to these words, to allow that we will never get the "whole story," that there will be blank patches, holes, moments of confusion. If commonplace books traditionally weave together a fabric of shared meaning, *No Common Place* tries to piece together a story made up of knots and tears.

Jared Stark

ACKNOWLEDGMENTS AND SOURCES

This book would not exist without the support of Cathy Caruth, who first introduced me to the Bacalls, and without the advice and encouragement of Geoffrey Hartman. Deep thanks are also due to Joanne Rudof, Dana Kline, and Susan Millen at the Fortunoff Video Archive for Holocaust Testimonies at Yale. Transcripts were prepared with care and persistence by Ed and Helen Silver at Silver Court Reporting, Pamela Levy, and Sophia Bacall-Cagan. For assistance with Polish words and phrases, I am indebted to Eliza Rechul, John Mackay, and Paul Rodel. Dina Abramowitz at the YIVO Jewish History Archive and Benjamin Meed of the Warsaw Ghetto Resistance Organization helped track down difficult references. Peter Antonuccio and Certified Video gave generously of their time and resources to prepare video stills. Alessia Ricciardi, Johannah Rodgers, Carra Hood, Eugenia Gomez-Escobar, Ulrich Baer, Raphael Gorospe, Catherine Dana, and Yitzhak Eisenberg thoughtfully commented on earlier versions of the text and provided crucial support and friendship throughout. Elaine Golin and Andres Batista were instrumental in the making of this book; they gave unreservedly of their time, intelligence, and warmth. The unstinting dedication of Armando Solis has touched every page and every day of this project. I owe more to my family—Rachel Stark and Ryan Lilienthal, Sidney and Sylvia Stark, and my parents Ellen and Albert—than I can possibly say. Finally, I am profoundly grateful to the entire Bacall family and to Ruth Fontak Kugelman, who with courage and commitment delved into their memories and archives for this book, and who took me into their family. To Alina, who trusted me with her story, I can only hope that this work repays her trust.

This work was partially funded by a grant from the Memorial Foundation for Jewish Culture, New York. For permission to reprint, we gratefully acknowledge the Fortunoff Video Archive for Holocaust Testimonies (T-2045, Alina Z.) at Yale University Library, *The New Jersey Jewish News*, and Kathleen Palm.

Jared Stark

Material for the notes and chronology is drawn from the following sources:

Yehuda Bauer, *A History of the Holocaust* (New York: Franklin Watts, 1982).

Michael Berenbaum, *The World Must Know: The History of the Holocaust as Told in the United States Holocaust Memorial Museum* (Boston: Little, Brown, and Company, 1993).

Danuta Czech, *Auschwitz Chronicle: 1939–1945* (New York: Henry Holt, 1990).

Debórah Dwork and Robert Jan Van Pelt, *Auschwitz: 1270 to the Present* (New York: W. W. Norton, 1996).

Angela Fiedermann, et al., *Das Konzentrationslager Mittelbau-Dora: Ein historischer Abriß* (Berlin: Westkreuz-Verlag, 1993).

Martin Gilbert, *The Holocaust* (London: Collins, 1986).

Israel Gutman, *Resistance: The Warsaw Ghetto Uprising* (Boston: Houghton Mifflin, 1994).

Raul Hilberg, *The Destruction of the European Jews* (Chicago, Quadrangle, 1961).

Eberhard Kolb, *Bergen-Belsen: From "Detention Center" to Concentration Camp, 1943–1945*, trans. Gregory Claeys and Christine Lattek (Göttingen: Vandenhoeck & Ruprecht, 1985).

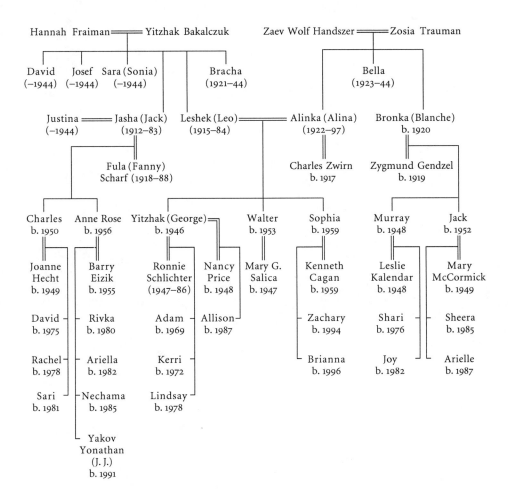

July 12, 1915

> *Birth of Leshek Bakalczuk, the fifth of six children, to parents*
> *Hannah and Yitzhak, in Davidgrodek, Poland (now Belarus).*

February 5, 1922

> *Birth of Alinka Handszer, the second of three daughters, to Zosia*
> *and Wolf (or Zaev Wolf), on Chmilna Street in Warsaw, Poland.*

September 1, 1939

> German invasion of Poland. Fall of Warsaw on September 27.

October 1940

> Establishment of the Warsaw ghetto.

November 15, 1940

> The gates of the Warsaw ghetto are closed after all non-Jews are
> moved outside of the ghetto borders and 183,000 Jews from other
> parts of Warsaw and the surrounding region are forced to move
> into the ghetto. Occupancy is estimated by a German official at
> 15.1 persons per apartment, or 6–7 per room.

September 7, 1941

> *Marriage of Alinka Handszer and Leshek Bakalczuk in the Warsaw*
> *ghetto.*

July 22, 1942

> Mass deportation of Warsaw Jews to Treblinka begins.

September 21, 1942

> Yom Kippur; 2,196 Jews are sent to Treblinka in the last of the
> series of massive deportations that began on July 22. Over a
> quarter of a million Jews, or three-quarters of the population of
> the Warsaw ghetto, were deported over the course of two months.
> The ghetto, formerly divided into two sections linked by a foot
> bridge, is reduced in size by more than half, thus eliminating the
> "small ghetto."
>
> *Leo and Alina are loaded onto a train destined for*
> *Treblinka. That night, they jump from the train twenty miles*
> *outside of Warsaw, near Tluszcz, and return to Warsaw the*
> *following day.*

April 19, 1943

The first night of Passover, and the first day of the Warsaw ghetto uprising. By the end of the first week of May, 631 resistance bunkers have been destroyed, and 30,000 Jews deported to concentration camps.

late April 1943

Leo and Alina are sent to the Majdanek death camp, near Lublin, Poland.

July 1, 1943

805 Jews from Majdanek arrive at Auschwitz, of whom 583 are women, given numbers 47632–48214.

Alina arrives in Auschwitz-Birkenau and is tattooed with an inverted triangle followed by the number 476490. It is not known why her tattoo ended with a 0.

July 11, 1943

1,331 Jews from Majdanek arrive at Auschwitz. The 763 men in the transport—including one who is already dead—are given numbers 128951–129713.

Leo arrives in Auschwitz-Birkenau and is tattooed with the number 129494 followed by an inverted triangle, which is recorded on his United States citizenship papers as the letter V.

early 1944

Leo is transferred from Auschwitz-Birkenau to Buna-Monowitz (part of the Auschwitz complex), where IG Farben used Jewish slave labor to build and run its synthetic rubber factory.

January 18, 1945

As Russian troops approach, the evacuation of all concentration camps in Upper Silesia begins, including Birkenau women's camp and Buna-Monowitz.

Alina begins three-day march from Auschwitz-Birkenau.

late January, 1945

Leo is evacuated from Buna-Monowitz. After a twenty-five-mile march to Gleiwitz and four days of waiting, he is loaded onto an open train car and sent to the Dora concentration camp and armaments factory, near Nordhausen, Germany.

January 20–22, 1945

For some Auschwitz evacuees, the "death march" ends at Wodzisław Śląski, thirty-five miles from the death camp. From there, open freight cars transport them to concentration camps including Gross-Rosen, Sachsenhausen, Ravensbrück,

Buchenwald, Mauthausen, and Bergen-Belsen. Others continue on foot in freezing conditions.

January 21, 1945

Alina is loaded on a train to Ravensbrück.

January 23–early February 1945

Transports of female prisoners from Auschwitz arrive at Ravensbrück.

mid-March 1945

Alina is transferred to a camp at Neustadt-Glewe, outside Lübeck, Germany.

April 4, 1945

Evacuation of Dora begins as American troops approach Nordhausen. Over 25,000 prisoners sent to Bergen-Belsen.

early April 1945

Leo is transferred to Bergen-Belsen.

April 15, 1945

British troops liberate Bergen-Belsen.

Leo is liberated, but sick with typhus, he remains at Bergen-Belsen.

May 2, 1945

American army reaches Neustadt-Glewe. Russian army arrives days later.

Alina is liberated at Neustadt-Glewe, Germany.

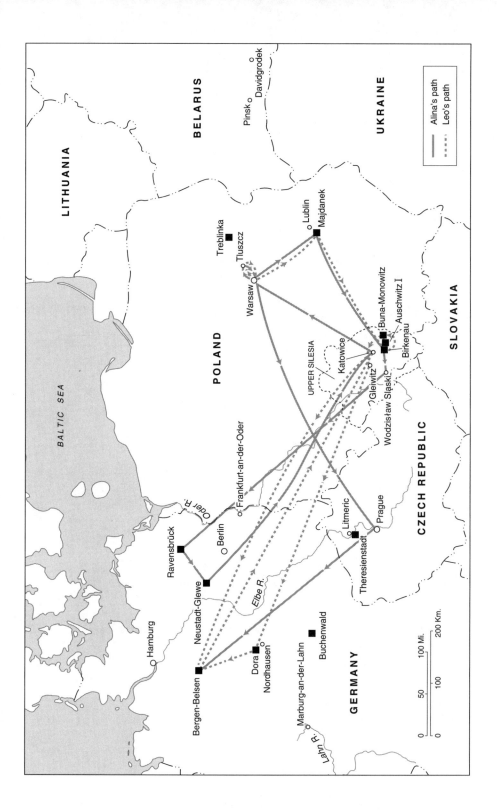

NOTE ON THE TEXT

Each excerpt is preceded by an indication of its source, given in italics. Asterisks (* * *) separate nonconsecutive portions of the same source. Each excerpt (unless noted with bracketed ellipses) is a continuous segment from the tape or text from which it is drawn.

Italicized excerpts or portions of excerpts are repeated from earlier in the book.

Ellipses (. . .) indicate pauses, hesitations, and interruptions that are part of the transcripts. Bracketed ellipses indicate editorial omissions.

No Common Place

The order of a book often means victory over oblivion.

How could we read a story studded with blank spaces?

It would quickly seem incomprehensible. We must appeal to recall,
give in to memory.

Do not neglect any trace. Note them all with care.

There are no detours—a detour is a hole in memory. Fear of the
unknown.

Lack. Lacuna.

A curve is but a straight line frightened by its own daring.

Reassuring image of the loop.

    Edmond Jabès, *The Book of Shares*, trans. Rosemarie Waldrop

I start preparing

evening of January 9, 1993
Tamarac, Florida

ALINA: That was before the holidays, just before the holidays, a few days, and before our New Year.

I start preparing, and buying and buying and buying for the holidays. Food, mostly. I'm buying food to eat.

And like, I feel, I don't know. I'm buying so much, sometimes I think that the war is coming. Any day it is going to break out and you have to prepare food.

I realize, you know . . . *nieświadomie* . . . I don't know how to say it . . . not knowing that . . . not knowing something happened to me, something is bothering me, and I really can't find, you know, I can't find the place, *i nie wiem* why.

I think I'm getting a cold, that I'm maybe sick. It is Friday, and it's only two days before the holiday, and I'm planning to cook for holiday. But I'm sitting by the table, and preparing mushrooms for the meat, and . . . and nobody is around me.

It's quiet, and my tears are coming so fast from my eyes. I don't know how to say in English, the tears coming from my eyes. Not coming, but *lecą* . . . like you run, so fast, coming from my eyes. And I can't stop. I'm crying, and crying, and all of a sudden, everything what I went through, my past, is coming before my eyes. You know, like *przelatują*, that means, *przelatują* like running, right? Running before my eyes. Can I say that? Running before my eyes.

And I'm making . . . and I feel I am terrible, terrible angry, and a lot of pain, and pain, and pain. And I'm thinking about the, you know, the Nazis, and I can't even . . . you know, I don't know why . . . I know why but . . . you know, they took . . .

I realize that I have my mother, my father before my eyes, my family, and they took away everybody. And they killed them, and they murdered them.

And my wedding in ghetto. I'm seeing me getting married. And my mother, and my father, and everybody looks hungry to me.

After I first spoke to Alina on the telephone in the fall of 1992, just before Rosh Hashanah of that year, Alina wrote down a series of reflections in Polish, in preparation for our meeting. Our first set of interviews took place a few months later, on January 8 and 9, 1993, mostly around the kitchen table of Alina's home in a retirement community in Tamarac, Florida, northwest of Ft. Lauderdale.

Alina's daughter, Sophia, was also present during these meetings, and after I had left them alone, Alina decided to translate her writing aloud, with a tape recorder running.

And uprising in Warsaw ghetto, and then trip to Treblinka, *gdzie* . . . you know, they want to . . . *gdzie chcieli nas za—* . . . Treblinka, where they want to kill us. They want to kill us, but we escape. And my jump with my husband from, from the train. And, and Leshek, you know, he was with me. And I don't know how to say it—*tortury*. *Tortury*, how you call it?

SOPHIA: Read the sentence.

ALINA: *Tortura* is: torture. In English it's torture, terrible torture. I don't know where I . . . what I have to . . .

SOPHIA: You went through terrible torture.

ALINA: Okay.

SOPHIA: *Tortury.*

ALINA: Yes. They took away from me my mother, my father, they killed my sister, the whole family. The whole family they murdered. And then, my wedding in the ghetto. And the uprising in Warsaw ghetto. And then a trip to Treblinka, where they want to kill us but we managed to escape, when we jumped from a train. And Leshek was with me, my husband was with me. And torture, and the torture.

Now I repeat myself. And the torture.

What I went through, the pains, the beating, and cold, and hungry. Why . . . *znaczy* . . . why me? Why my husband? Why the family? Why? I . . . I'm sitting . . .

Why me? Why, you know, why my . . . I'm sitting, and I realize how terrible, terrible it was.

And they kill my baby too.

I'm peeling the mushrooms for the holiday, yet I hate the holiday. Why I'm preparing everything? I'm asking the question. Why I'm preparing everything? For whom? I hate the holiday. Hitler, the bandit, he murdered us in every holiday, in each holiday. I am so bitter, I'm so angry. I can't take it.

And I can't stop crying. I myself wonder why, *gdyż ja* . . . *ja*, I, *ja nie, ja nie mogłam* . . . I couldn't, I couldn't cry. When I want, I couldn't cry, my tears never came out of my eyes. And all of a sudden I can't stop. And, and that was for years. I miss terrible my kids and my children.

SOPHIA: It's okay, mommy. It's okay, mommy.

ALINA: I miss so terrible my children. That's all what I have, what's left. I am very much . . . I very much appreciate. Terrible . . . missing . . . crying . . . Leshek . . . It's worse than my anger.

Nie mogę prze— . . . I can't stop crying and I'm crying for the six million *co nie* . . . what . . . what . . . what should, should not, *co nie powinni byli zginąć* . . . what they not supposed to die, they're not supposed to . . . *zginąć* . . . get lost, you know, not to . . .

SOPHIA: Be forgotten.

ALINA: . . . be forgotten . . . *ze świata*. They shouldn't disappear from the world.

Why they kill my first baby, my first son?

This is not to understand.

I . . . I can't understand.

I can't believe.

This is terrible. But *niestety jest to okropna prawda* . . . this is terrible truth. This is *okropna prawda*. How you say? This is . . .

SOPHIA: Terrible truth.

ALINA: This is terrible, this is terrible truth.

* * *

ALINA: That's it. I even didn't know that I was reading, when I was so angry.

SOPHIA: Keep going.

ALINA: That's it. I feel I'm going to write more.

SOPHIA: It's beautiful.

ALINA: Hmm?

SOPHIA: You did a good job.

ALINA: You think so?

SOPHIA: Excellent.

ALINA: But this is not . . .

SOPHIA: It's your feelings. How could it be any . . .

ALINA: But this is not what I felt. I couldn't stop crying. And, and when I start crying, I got very angry.

SOPHIA: You got angry at yourself for crying, you mean?

ALINA: No. Angry what happened to me.

Alina has finished translating, but she and Sophia leave the tape recorder on.

* * *

Why I'm preparing everything? I'm asking a question. Why I'm preparing everything? For whom?

* * *

SOPHIA: *You got angry at yourself for crying, you mean?*

ALINA: *No. Angry what happened to me.*

SOPHIA: That's okay. There's nothing wrong with that. It's about time. Seventy years of holding it in is a long time.

ALINA: And I wonder, I wonder because I couldn't cry for years.

[3]

SOPHIA: Well, now it's coming out. It's nice to hear your feelings. It's something I've always known inside but never heard.

morning of January 9, 1993
Tamarac
JARED STARK: How did you feel listening to your mother yesterday?

SOPHIA: Emotional. I kept thinking all these years that I knew inside what happened; and I knew some of the stories, not because I asked them or not because I was told them, but only sometimes during the holidays or when my parents had company over, especially other survivors, they would start talking about their accounts in the ghetto and their accounts in concentration camps. My father would basically talk about it a lot more than my mother. My mother would get angry at my father, and he would start talking about it almost like therapy, every day. It got to the point where people didn't want to hear it any more. But I would sit there with eyes open, and listening and listening because I wanted to get out as much as I could. Too afraid to ask questions, because I didn't want them . . . As much as I wanted to hear about it, I didn't want them to get upset about it. So I never asked the questions I wanted to ask.

As Alina began to tell her story, Sophia found herself asking questions she had never asked before. It was she who had first invited me to meet her mother and who, of Alina's family, participated most actively in this project.

evening of January 9, 1993
Tamarac
SOPHIA: Just keep talking . . .

ALINA: This here, is not clear over there. Why you push two? Here is like, that's all what's left for me, you know, my children, that's what is . . . *zostało* . . . how you say it? Left over . . .

SOPHIA: That's all I have left.

ALINA: That's all what I have left, that's all what I have left. I have to change that.

SOPHIA: Explain that you want to expand on that point, that your children are all that you have left.

ALINA: My children, yes . . . but this is something no good. You're stopping here . . .

SOPHIA: You're recording, you push two to record.

ALINA: Now?

SOPHIA: Yes, you're on the tape. Explain what you want to explain.

ALINA: Oh, I see. I didn't understand . . .

Sophia teaches Alina that two buttons, play and record, must be pressed on the tape recorder in order to record.

* * *

ALINA: You know, it's not clear what I want to say. It's hard to translate it from Polish to English. What I want to say is that I miss very much, especially when the holidays come. I always have my children with me, and, and I miss them very much. I miss the kids, and that's all what I have left, and I am, and I am very much appreciate for it. I'm very appreciate what I have.

Alina and Sophia begin to wind up their conversation.

The rest I said, yes? I said, they shouldn't disappear from this world, the whole family, did I say that? And this is not, not to understand.

I want to say, *nie do uwierzenia* . . . it's hard to believe, you know, hard to believe what happened to us, not only to me and to my family. But right now I have my family before me. My . . . everybody who was murdered, and why? I still can't understand. It's not to understand. And it's not to believe. But I'm sorry to say this is terrible truth. This is terrible truth.

Alina turns again to her notes and retranslates a few sentences.

I'm going to shut off this, I'm going to close now for a while. It's late, you have to get up in the morning and go. I don't want to . . .

SOPHIA: I want to hear it.

ALINA: But I don't want you . . .

SOPHIA: I want to hear it.

ALINA: It's not for before you go to sleep.

2

Until there is company

January 11, 1993

Dear Jared,

Hope your trip home was uneventful! I wanted to thank you for coming to meet my mom and making her feel comfortable. She liked you and the way you handled this very "emotional situation." We are confident in you and hope it all works out great for all. Enclosed is another tape that mom did the night before I left. It is the translation of words she wrote in Polish. Very touching, very emotional and as you can tell I just let the tape go—so keep listening. Call me with your thoughts.

When I later asked Alina for a copy of her Polish text, she was unable to locate it.

Fondly,

Sophia

February 3, 1993

New Haven, Connecticut

Dear Sophia,

I'm sorry I have not written sooner, but the semester took off to a quick start, and has not yet slowed down its pace. I did want to confirm, however, my receipt of the cassette you recorded with your mother. I hope she continues to use the tape recorder as a way of experimenting with different approaches to expressing her thoughts, her memories, her history. I cannot tell you how moved— and impressed—I was by her narrative abilities. [. . .]

I'm also enclosing with this note a copy of the tapes from Friday, Jan. 8. Do you want to (can you) transcribe them? I'm in no hurry . . . but if you'd like to give it a go . . .

I'd also like to try to schedule a visit for your mother to the Holocaust Video Archives here, so when you know her travel schedule (roughly), she or you can call or write me.

"Charlie" is Charles Zwirn, whom Alina married in 1990, six years after Leo's death.

It was wonderful meeting you both and Charlie, and it helped me conceive of this project as a real, and compelling, possibility.

Yours,

Jared

[6]

Bakalczuk family in 1925 (left to right): Leo's brothers Josef and David; his mother, Hannah; his sisters, Sara (Sonia) and Bracha; his brother Jasha; his father, Yitzhak; and Leshek (Leo), age ten.

summer 1993

Hi Jared!

Hope upon receipt of this letter you are fine, over your exams and rested! Is that possible?

Enclosed you will find Mom's interview tape from Florida. It turned out to be approximately 16 pages. Not bad. Even after being there when you interviewed her, I still can't comprehend all that she and my father went through. [. . .]

I typed this interview just like mom spoke. I hope this is what you wanted and that it makes sense to you. Call me upon receipt of it so we may discuss it. Good luck Jared!

Very truly yours,

Sophia B. Cagan

January 8, 1993

Tamarac

SOPHIA: How are you doing, Mom?

ALINA: I am doing okay, because I am alive and I thought I would never be alive to have family, to have children, and to be a grandma, to have grandchildren. This is something that I treasure. And that's the only thing I'm not complaining . . . I'm happy.

I went through, was a terrible experience for me, for everybody, and it was a long time after that I didn't want to have even a child, because I lost one. And I was afraid that's going to happen again.

I came from a small family. I had two sisters. My husband had six brothers, together six, you know, four brothers and two sisters, six. And he said, I hope now we can have a family, and he was always pushing, you know. I was for a long time thinking about, could happen again. And I'm afraid.

I see what's going on. After what we went through, can you imagine, it's happening again and again. In Yugoslavia, what they're killing people again. For what? Because they are Muslim?

April 21, 1993
New Haven
T-2045, Alina Z., Fortunoff Video Archive for Holocaust Testimonies, *Yale University Library*
Interviewers: Dana Kline and Susan Millen

ALINA: I was worried about my children a lot, if they're going to grow up to be normal children. A lot, because was always crying in the house, especially for holidays. And it was hard with us together. That's what I was worried about.

I didn't come with anything. Very little I was talking what I went through. I was afraid to tell it. But my husband was the talker. He was talking and talking and telling them everything. And I said, wait, let them grow up.

But they know.

January 9, 1993
Tamarac

JARED: When did you first have a sense of what had happened to your parents?

SOPHIA: I'm real bad with that. I'm real bad with times and stuff. I kind of associated a lot with people who were adopted as children and they sort of just know it. They're told it at a very young age. They're not told it . . . parents tell the child about their adoption and they kind of talk about it. In this sense it was different. My parents never told me of their stories, but from a very young age I remember hearing little bits and pieces of it.

ALINA: You were asking if you were adopted.

SOPHIA: I did? What year?

ALINA: When you was very young, really. I didn't know why she asked if she was adopted. I used to joke. I said, I'm your mother a hundred percent, but the daddy is never sure.

[8]

March 15, 1994

Tamarac

ALINA: One letter I remember, what Sophia wrote.

JARED: To you?

ALINA: No, to somebody who wrote they don't believe what happened. And she wrote him a letter. You have the letter? Yes? When she mentioned, what you think? My father, mother wants to be popular that they put the number on that . . . tattoos on their hand? Remember the letter what she wrote?

JARED: Yes, I do.

ALINA: And then, I didn't have a grandma who will put handkerchief over my head. And remember this letter?

JARED: The letter is in the book.

ALINA: In the book?

JARED: Yes, the one that you're reading.

ALINA: Yes?

JARED: Yes.

ALINA: And that's, you know, that's everything comes to my head, and everything. If you raise the kids, you know, you don't realize that they didn't have easy lives. Same with me. Every holiday they was sitting, looking at my, my husband. I fought with him . . . I . . . you know . . .

And my husband used to talk a lot about it. And I was angry always. I was so angry.

I said, don't talk. I don't want . . . I want my children to be, you know, to be grown up in healthy, healthy atmosphere. You have time to tell them, I said, when they going to be older.

And he cry when he dine. He cry. He couldn't help it, you know, because of his past. Every holiday he read the book, Hebrew book, he make Kaddish. Or happy occasion, he cry.

But he live to be witness to happy occasion. And always he wasn't such a . . .

JARED: He cried about his happiness?

ALINA: Yes. Me too. Me too, sometimes. When I'm happy, I can cry, I get started. When I'm happy, I'm not happy. It takes time, you know, later on.

JARED: Really?

ALINA: That's how they start with me. If I'm happy, I'm not showing so much, like, later on, it comes on.

My second set of interviews with Alina took place in March of 1994, again in Florida. Sophia, seven months pregnant with her first child, remained at home in Connecticut.

I had given Alina an early draft of this chapter, but she had not yet had a chance to read it.

Alina, Leo, Sophia, Walter, and George Bacall. Bloomfield, Connecticut, 1983. Courtesy Kathleen Palm.

Or crying. I can't cry in the beginning. Like tragedy, I cannot cry, but later on I can. It's coming to me.

So . . . and I have beautiful children. But they suffer, because of us.

January 5, 1978
The Jewish News
East Orange, New Jersey
To the Editor:
Sir—I am 18 years old and a daughter of parents who were concentration camp victims. I am writing to you to comment on your article "What Did Happen to the Six Million?" in the Dec. 15, 1977, issue of *The Jewish News.*

Sophia's letter appeared under the headline "It's the Truth."

I was never more furious in all my life, not even when my parents (Mr. and Mrs. Leon Bacall) would tell me of what and how they suffered! It was infuriating to read and realize that people don't believe the Holocaust ever took place.

How can these people assume these lies?

Perhaps I am taking things too far, or maybe these people don't really understand because they did not go through it themselves, but if people can believe in all the people that got killed in Vietnam, in the Six Day War in Israel, they should at least say to themselves, "Well, maybe, just maybe, the Holocaust did exist at one time or other."

Nobody, but nobody, can tell me that there was no Holocaust, with the pain I see my parents go through, the tears and sickness at holidays or just any day of the week.

I will not even mention the hard times, because I know the pain they have suffered, and have to wait until there is company to find out some of the tragedies which occurred.

How can these people say, "Auschwitz? A fraud," "Treblinka? A lie!" If it is a lie, or just assume it, then where did my grandparents go? My uncles and aunts, and yes, even a brother?

Are these lies? No, they are not! I don't have grandparents to go to on holidays, to make me scarves, to watch over me. I have none of these things, none!

Hitler and his damn Nazis did these things. No one can tell me different.

Would my parents waste four years trying to get a book written? Why did they jump from a train going 70 miles an hour? Only to prove to the people, no matter race, nationalities or ages, that people like the Nazis existed. Yet people like my parents are strong, and strength and faith are the only thing that kept them going!

My parents have tattoos of numbers on their arms. I sit and watch every day, and there's not a second that goes by where I don't see them suffering. You tell me, would they go and have numbers tattooed on their arms to be popular?

This letter should prove to some people out there that the Holocaust is no joke, not a fantasy but a reality. If you print this letter, it really should help people realize that they should think before they talk!

My parents do not know I am writing this letter and I can only pray they will see that at least their children understand, my two brothers, Walter and Dr. George Bacall, and myself, if this is printed.

I have never seen an article from the children of concentration

The book Sophia refers to here is "One Small Candle," the unpublished manuscript prepared in the early 1970s by a freelance writer, Lawrence Murphy. By the time Sophia wrote this letter it was becoming clear that the manuscript would never be published.

camp victims in *The Jewish News*. Will you please, not for me, but for people out there, non-believers, print this letter?

If you do not print this at least let me know what you feel. Thank you, for at least listening. I am just plain upset about hearing of people not believing. It is not fair. The Holocaust did exist.

Sophie A. Bacall

Morristown

January 9, 1993
Tamarac

SOPHIA: I didn't want them to get upset about it, so I never asked the questions I wanted to ask. So to hear my mother the other night I was very proud of her and what she was doing. And finally realizing that the reason that she survived was to tell the story. And she's telling the story now.

* * *

JARED: So how did you feel about talking yesterday?

ALINA: Very good. I was very good. I think if nothing else, knowing I had a little on my conscience, because I'm not speaking out about my experience in concentration camp. Because everybody had their own little story for themselves. And I think — I don't know why — but I think I was the only one what went through a hell, more than anybody else, I don't know why. What I have, I went being pregnant . . .

JARED: Were you scared about talking, before we talked yesterday? How did you feel before I came over?

ALINA: I wasn't scared. I was not even thinking about what's going to be. I just decided to go with my information to give to the world, that's it. I want my children to remember when I'm not around. I don't want to hide anything. I want them to know, and it's a small family so it's very important. So I feel great that I decided to talk about it.

Who will remember

3

January 13, 1985
Kathleen Palm, "Who Will Remember Our Stories?"
Northeast Magazine
The Hartford Courant

Who will remember our stories? Leo Bacall's recollections are remarkable for their candor and their insight into the darkest time in human history. The Holocaust had taught him courage. Yet before he died, Leo Bacall feared one thing: that his children would not know what had happened—that the world would not know what had happened.

April 21, 1993
New Haven
Fortunoff Video Archive at Yale

ALINA: I have here an article, this is *Northeast Magazine*. A friend of my son, George Bacall, she's a very beautiful person, she was very interested in our history. She was asking, and my husband was alive, and he was always talking what we went through, and she was very interested. So when we were like sitting shivah, when he died, in George's house, my son's house, she decided to write about the story.

January 8, 1993
Tamarac

ALINA: I want my husband to appear as a hero because I stayed alive only because of him. He was brave and he helped me a lot. He was a hero because when he went with me, I saw a lot of husbands run away from their wives. But he said, I don't have any life without me.

January 13, 1985
The Hartford Courant

"At the station, they said some of the men need not go," Leo said, "for there was still work to be done in the Ghetto."

[13]

Alina begged him to stay.

"I hoped for a witness," Alina said, "but he would not leave me."

March 15, 1994
Tamarac

ALINA: I beg him, I beg him, you know, when they closed up the streets. You know, that's the system of them. They close up one street, and they scream, and they say, everybody down, everybody down. And when you're down, because they're looking in each apartment and shooting under the beds and everything . . .

So when we went down, they said, men could stay and women have to go. So my husband, when he came down, he took tools. What kind of tools? I think files.

And I said, I beg him, I say, goodbye, you stay, maybe you're going to stay alive. Maybe you're going to stay alive. Because I never believed we were going to work or someplace like this.

But then he said to me, I cannot live without you, I have to go with you. But in his head was already to jump from the train.

Lawrence Murphy, "One Small Candle: The True Story of Alina and Leo Bacall" (unpublished manuscript), p. 34

They burst into our room at once. They broke down the door of the apartment with the stocks of their machine guns.

They lined us up against the wall of the apartment and searched us, then ordered us out of the building. We went down the stairs not knowing if we would make it to the street.

Out in the night, troops guarded a group of about 200. They organized us into a column and marched us through the streets of the Walled City.

They announced that men need not go, that there was still work for us to do in the Walled City and my wife, Alina, begged me to stay behind. She hoped for a witness. I WOULD NOT LEAVE HER.

January 5, 1978
The Jewish News
Why did they jump from a train going 70 miles an hour?

March 15, 1994
Tamarac
JARED: When you told me this once before, or maybe it was in the book, you didn't only say to Leo, stay and stay alive. You also said, stay to tell my story.

ALINA: Yes. If I told him stay, and be a witness what happened, tell the story, that's the same thing. Stay alive.

Because I believe that he's going to be alive, and my sister going to be alive, and who else? That's it. My sister and my husband. The two are going to be alive, because my sister was on the Gentile side. And my husband look like German. He was lucky.

When he came to concentration camp, they gave him a good job. He was blonde with blue eyes. I felt like he could make it, you know? He could probably make it. That's why I said, stay here, maybe you're going to be alive and can tell the story what happened. A witness.

And he said, no, I cannot live without you, I go with you.

4 I remember not too much

June 1993
letter from Sophia to Jared

Enclosed you will find my Mom's testimon[y] from Yale. I watched it the other night and my reaction was disbelief. Even though I had been there when she was taping the video, I guess I was more worried about mom making it through it than listening as intently as I did the other night. Jared, after all these years, my reaction is I cannot believe they made it. A 17-year-old girl and a 24-year-old man. What strength!

Sophia gives her parents' ages in 1939, the year Poland was invaded.

My mom also called me the morning after she saw the tape. She states that she cried all the way through it. Her reaction was the same. She said that after hearing what she said, herself, she couldn't believe they made it.

April 21, 1993
New Haven
Fortunoff Video Archive at Yale

DANA: Dana Kline. This is the Yale Video Archive for Holocaust Testimonies. Today is April the twenty-first, 1993.

SUSAN: Susan Millen.

ALINA: My name is Alina Bakalczuk.

DANA: And where were you born?

ALINA: I was born in Warsaw, in Poland, on February 5, 1922. And I remember not too much, because I lost a lot of my memory, especially the numbers, years. I'm trying hard to remember whatever I could.

March 15, 1994
Tamarac

ALINA: Do you know, it's a funny thing, I speak better today . . .

JARED: Than when?

ALINA: Than by myself. I get nervous. And funny thing, I don't remember things from yesterday, but some things I remember good

from what I went through. I'm getting older, the memory's not so good anymore, I'm afraid I'm going to forget a lot of things.

I will not remember the numbers. This I block when I go out from concentration camp[. . .]How is it that I don't remember? I don't remember the number of the block what I was in concentration camp.

JARED: Why do you think you don't remember?

ALINA: I don't know. Not only now, before too. Like I block out everything. I didn't want to remember. Something happened in my brain, I don't know. Because I act different than anybody else when I find out I'm free.

JARED: Do you remember the number you had on your arm?

ALINA: I don't remember . . . forty-nine, I remember. I have it on citizen papers.

JARED: But you don't remember the whole thing?

ALINA: I probably don't want to know. I don't remember the number, I don't remember the block number.

January 9, 1993
Tamarac
JARED: What was your maiden name?

ALINA: Handszer. H-A-N-D-S-Z-E-R. Sounds like a German name.

Zosia Handszer and her eldest daughter, Bronka, 1926.

JARED: And your father's name?

ALINA: Wolf, and my mother's name Zosia. But my father used to call her Zisela . . .

SOPHIA: You used to call me that.

ALINA: Zisela, it's like, sweet. I don't know why he called her Zisela but this was like, if you like somebody, if you love somebody, like you call love to somebody, my love. But he used to call her Zisela . . .

* * *

ALINA: She was a beautiful person. I used to call her angel, always angel. She was so good, she always made peace in the family, you know? My mother, like me, I try the same thing. It's very important.

SOPHIA: Mom, you're describing yourself.

ALINA: What?

SOPHIA: You're describing yourself.

ALINA: Maybe.

A WAITRESS: Would you like me to wrap this up?

ALINA: Yes, thank you.

SOPHIA: Is it okay if we sit here a while?

WAITRESS: Yes, you're fine there.

ALINA: So that's what I remember.

JARED: And your father?

ALINA: My father was always busy, he was a sick man, he was very busy. And he was nervous. He's a good man, good family, but he

Part of our discussion took place over lunch and coffee at a local delicatessen.

was . . . I remember my mother, you know, when he talked loud.

Like, I remember, was accident with my sister. She came home with the guys, and daddy said that one of the guys was drunk. And he came home, and he make such a stink out of it, you know? With my mother, because Blanche . . .

WAITRESS: Would you like some more coffee?

ALINA: Do you want some more coffee? No, thanks. And this I will never forget.

* * *

ALINA: And when I start going out with my husband . . . he wants to go with me, was like, in the park, was dancing for young people, music, and you could have coffee . . . we didn't have coffee, but this was something like a sour milk, this was something, *Milchkaffee*, and we have something, and we danced, and that was something like buttermilk, like buttermilk, and this was a luxury, you see?

And he asked me, my husband asked me, at what time you have to be home?

And I didn't want to tell him that eight o'clock I have to be home. I said, don't worry.

And eleven o'clock, when he drove me home, my mother was very angry. And she said to Blanche, I will kill her, she said.

And Blanche was waiting for me, she was afraid my mother was going to kill me. And she called me.

I came home, and my mother said, I'm not going to talk to you now, it's late. I talk to you tomorrow.

* * *

ALINA: And I said to my mother, you want me to be eight o'clock, I could go out with him eight o'clock.

So she asked my sister, what happened to Alinka?

She said, oh ma, she met a good-looking guy.

So my mother knew I'm going out with someone. So she said to me . . . but I never want to invite my husband because he was seven years older, I was afraid my father would throw him out, he's too old for my daughter. So I never invite him.

But my mother told me, I let you stay longer if you introduce him to me, I want to know with whom you're going out.

I said, all right. So I introduce him, and my mother fell in love with him because she didn't have a boy, only three girls. She loves him.

* * *

ALINA: I remember it was a holiday, ocean . . . how do you call it when you have a holiday what you celebrate the water, the ocean, you have that something here?

JARED: To celebrate the ocean?

SOPHIA: Like the Fourth of July?

ALINA: Like Fourth of July . . . You know, you throwing flowers to the water, some kind of holiday like this, I don't remember the name . . . *Swieto-morza*, that's what it is, Holiday of the Sea. And I make a date with him to go there, and you have to walk and walk and walk. You don't have the ten *groszy* for the trolley car, are you kidding? You have to walk.

We walk, and I tell him . . . you know that her name was Rilka. You see, I remember the names when I was young. And I said, you know? She's in love with you, she's a nice girl, and I would love you to go out with her.

And he looked at me, and said, I love you!

And I said, but I don't love you.

That's what started that. A funny thing, we start to talk, and I like him very much, when daddy starts to talk, and he says, I can't help it. I fall in love from the first time, he said.

How could you fall in love? You even don't know me good. But he was older than I was, seven years older. You know, at this time I was like a child compared to him.

And I came back and I told her, Rilka, he don't love you, and he love me, you know, like that. And I can't help it.

So she said, okay, I can't help myself, he loves you.

And I remember the second time I went out with daddy, and I will never forget, daddy brought me a manicure set, of red leather, beautiful. And he gave it to me. And I said, oh no, I'm not going to give him back that. It was so beautiful, I was dying to have it. I came home, you know, I was like a child, I put this under my bed, my mother shouldn't see it.

April 21, 1993
New Haven
Fortunoff Video Archive at Yale

ALINA: I met my husband in 1939, and in 1941, in September, we got married.

DANA: You were in the ghetto then?

ALINA: Yes, that was the ghetto, that was already the small ghetto.

* * *

ALINA: I don't know how you call this here. I think high school, right? I was in second year when the war broke out. That was vacation time, but we went to school, like, you know, to meet each other, and we hear they bombing Warsaw. And we thought, that's nothing. We didn't expect that.

And that is what starts. And our home was bombed, completely. And lucky we stay alive, my mother and my father, and we moved to our aunt and uncle apartment. A small apartment. I remember I was sleeping on the table with my sister. It was a small, like a studio apartment. And my older sister, she run to, on Russian side, because she was afraid of Germany, so she went to Russia.

DANA: Your older sister left?

ALINA: My oldest, yes. But she came back. She could not stay there.

From over there, after the war, I don't remember the year, but I think a year later, they started to close us up in the ghetto. '41, was already the wall around.

DANA: Do you remember moving in?

ALINA: Yes.

DANA: Could you describe that to us?

ALINA: They just tell us that we have to move from the Gentile side. They tell you what street belong to us. And we were looking, and we were finding somebody who wants to change with us. We were changing the apartment. I remember the first apartment was on Electoralna Street, yes. We lived there for a short time, and they said we had to move, this belonged to the . . . and they were making the ghetto smaller and smaller. We used to have in Warsaw two ghettos, small ghetto and large ghetto. That was terrible . . . hunger.

And again, I remember my mother, you know, we were so hungry, and my younger sister swell up from hunger, but we didn't want my mother should feel bad about it so we put the record player, and we dance and we sing, that our mother shouldn't worry about us. We want her to believe that we're not hungry.

And I don't know how she got a little fish, what they're called, smelts, fish? I don't know from where. And she said to me, Alinka— she called me Alinka—take this and bring this to my sister, to Aunt Rose, her name was Rose.

I looked at her, and I said, my gosh, I am hungry, she is hungry, everybody's hungry, and she managed to cook something for her sister, not for us. But when I came over there and saw my aunt with

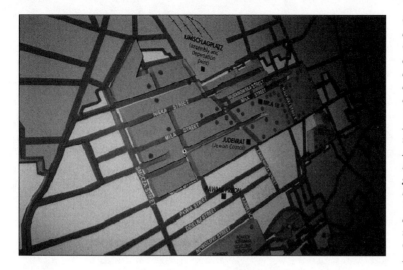

On April 22 and 23, 1993, Alina, George, Sophia, and I attended the dedication ceremonies and the opening day of the U.S. Holocaust Memorial Museum in Washington DC. Alina talked about her time in the ghetto as we stood by a map of the Warsaw ghetto on display in the museum. Courtesy George Bacall.

the three or four children in the bed, they were starving from hunger. Skeletons.

April 23, 1993
U.S. Holocaust Memorial Museum
Washington DC

ALINA: Where's Zamenhofa? Do you see Zamenhofa there? Where the army walked . . .

JARED: Here's Zamenhofa, right there.

ALINA: I used to live here . . .

SOPHIA: There it is, Zamenhofa Street.

GEORGE: Zamenhofa, Mila . . . It crosses Mila.

ALINA: And where is Muranowska? Over there . . .

SOPHIA: Right there.

ALINA: There, for a long time we were there.

JARED: Muranowska and Zamenhofa?

ALINA: Yes, and what is this street higher?

JARED: Niska.

ALINA: Niska, yes, and then?

JARED: No name.

GEORGE: That's the *Umschlagplatz*.

ALINA: Niska, it was there our bunker.

GEORGE: On Niska?

ALINA: Yes. And here's where we got married, on Nowolipki Street, here.

Umschlagplatz: *loading area for freight trains in Warsaw, used to load Jews onto cattle cars bound for concentration and death camps. Literally, transfer point.*

January 13, 1985
The Hartford Courant
Alina's family had to move into the ghetto. Leo and his brother Jack, with a few other young men, immediately devised ways to smuggle food to the people there. They were clever and for a long time were not detected, but one day as they returned home they were beaten by soldiers in the street under the window while their father watched. Two weeks later their father was dead, Leo said, of a broken heart.

"We were married six weeks after that," said Alina. "The date had been chosen and the tradition said you must not change it once it was set. You must also serve cake and wine at a wedding, so my mother sold her coat to buy some. Both families were mourning, but my mother would not break the tradition."

March 16, 1994
Tamarac
ALINA: And I said, everybody was in black dresses—which was true, because we didn't have anything to wear.

January 9, 1993
Tamarac
ALINA: In Warsaw, like I was in Warsaw, the daughter married, she used to live three streets away, two streets away. And the family always was very close, especially the parents was Jews. I couldn't believe I was going to live without my mother, and I was seventeen.

To the end, it's a different story

5

January 13, 1985
The Hartford Courant
"They would attack us always during the holidays of the tradition because that was another way they thought to destroy it," Leo said.

"One Small Candle," p. 34
It was while we were celebrating our day of forgiveness, when Alina and I were taken.

They burst into our room at once. They broke down the door of the apartment with the stocks of their machine guns. They lined us up against the wall of the apartment and searched us, then ordered us out of the building.

January 13, 1985
The Hartford Courant
In Warsaw, in the spring of 1942, he said, as he and Alina observed the Passover, the storm troopers with machine guns broke down the door of their little room at No. 5 Dr. Zamenhoff Street in the Ghetto. Alina and Leo held each other close.

March 15, 1994
Tamarac
ALINA: He put not in Yom Kippur, I think he put this on another holiday.

JARED: He put it on Yom Kippur. The newspaper article put it on Passover.

ALINA: Yes, that's right. This is like telling stories. So from mouth to mouth to the end, it's a different story.

Alina alerts me to an error in the Hartford Courant article but attributes it to the unpublished manuscript, "One Small Candle."

"One Small Candle," p. 35
People were being herded into the train depot and we saw them marching by torchlight. All had been taken in scattered raids. They encompassed the street like a pilgrimage of the faithful, all bound together with a common destination, a common faith and a common

Although "One Small Candle" correctly records that Alina and Leo were first taken from the Warsaw ghetto on Yom Kippur, 1942, it superimposes the image of the Exodus, part of the Passover story, onto the story of their deportation.

goal. It was an organized Exodus in reverse. Our Promised Land was lost, the end was at hand, and we shared not hope, but rumors.

April 21, 1993
New Haven
Fortunoff Video Archive at Yale

ALINA: I don't remember if the same year or a year later, this I really . . . terrible . . . Maybe I find in writing, or in our book, because my husband remembered more than I.

It was Yom Kippur, and they were looking, my husband was looking something to find, that we should have something for the holiday. So he went with his friends outside the house, on the street to look for something. I don't know for what they were looking. People were dying on the street, we could see it.

And he finds a dead horse this time. And they cut off a piece of meat and he brought home, and he said, cook that for the holiday.

And I cook, and we never were able to eat, because they closed up our street and took us all downstairs, and put us in cattle train, and they were taking us to Treblinka.

March 15, 1994
Tamarac

JARED: What time of day was it?

ALINA: That was in daytime, but we jumped in the middle of the night.

JARED: So it was the day of Yom Kippur, or the day before?

ALINA: The food was ready to eat before fasting, okay? And the same night we jumped, in Yom Kippur. It was in Yom Kippur.

JARED: You were rounded up during dinner, during your pre-fast meal?

ALINA: Yes, and how! I told you how we made the dinner, was a dead horse on the street, you remember? And I remember we made pea soup. This I will never forget, pea soup. And I make hamburger, I think, from the meat. And we didn't eat, we didn't manage to eat anything.

evening of January 9, 1993
Tamarac
I'm buying so much that I think, sometimes I think that the war should, is coming, any day going to break out and you have to prepare food.

[26]

July 11, 1994

West Hartford, Connecticut

ALINA: They decide to go on the street and see maybe they could get some food to make the dinner before fasting, something to eat. And matter of fact, we fast all the time, but it's like a tradition, you know, to make something to have, sitting by the table, and then you don't eat the next, like, for twenty-four hours. And while walking on the street they saw a dead horse, and they start to cut a piece of meat, and they brought me meat, and I made hamburger . . .

JARED: Tell me how you made it.

ALINA: How I made? I put whatever I have home. I don't remember what I have. It was very hard to make anything. Grind the meat, and whatever I have home I put. If I have eggs, I put eggs. If I have matzoh meal, I put matzoh meal, like bread crumbs. And, and I fry in a little oil. So I remember I had this.

JARED: What kind of oil?

ALINA: We used to have only one oil, or chicken fat, whatever. I still, I don't remember what I put in the hamburger. Plain meat, maybe. And then I made pea soup. I remember we had peas, and I made pea soup.

JARED: How did you make the pea soup?

ALINA: I put the peas, I wash the peas, and then put in the water and boil, that's it. And you put garlic to taste, salt to taste. In Europe we used to put farfalle. I don't know, we didn't have that. But that soup was plain. Just peas and lot of water.

JARED: What did you put in Europe?

ALINA: A lot of water.

JARED: No . . . farfalle?

ALINA: Pasta, dry pasta, but I don't think we had that. Usually my mother used to put.

And then I sat, everything was ready on the table, and we didn't start eating. We hear everybody should come down. The German came, the Nazi came, and scream to us, everybody have to go. They close up certain streets, like a section, you know, of Warsaw, like one street from both sides. And we have to go down.

March 15, 1994

Tamarac

JARED: So it was only you and Leo at dinner? No one else was with you?

In July 1994 I met Alina when she was visiting her family in Connecticut. It was Sophia's first day at work since the birth of her first son, Zachary. Alina and I talked while she happily took care of the baby at her son George's house.

[27]

ALINA: Oh, yes, friends. I have five couples together. We were my friend with her husband—from school friend—and her husband's brother, and sister. So one, two, three, four, five, six I think was there.

JARED: Six people?

ALINA: Six people.

JARED: And you were all taken together?

ALINA: Yes. And they all got killed.

* * *

ALINA: My parents was still alive, because after that they came, and they saw everything on the table, and they knew. So my mother called out to my sister and said, Alinka is not alive anymore.

She called me Alinka, you know.

A small opening

6

April 21, 1993
New Haven
Fortunoff Video Archive at Yale

ALINA: I didn't have any help from anybody. I was hiding, I was scared, especially when we jumped from a train and we didn't have a place where to go. We are free, we are not in Treblinka to be killed, and we didn't have any place to go.

* * *

ALINA: You know, we were with our friends from school, all young people. And the whole wagon was so many people, young people.

And we told them . . . because when my husband . . . they put our train on the side and they were waiting for the middle of the night to start us to move. And my husband saw a guy who took care of the station, and he ask him, could you tell me where we are going?

And he said, if you could, save yourself, because you are going to Treblinka, to death camp.

DANA: Did you ever hear of Treblinka before?

ALINA: No. You know, some people used to receive letters, cards, that they are working, you know. The only thing, very late we find out that they killing us. I didn't think about gas or something like this. And then you get experience.

January 8, 1993
Tamarac

ALINA: There were my schoolgirl friends. One was married and the other one was like a sister of my friend's husband, so we were another two couples, three couples altogether.

My husband took a handkerchief and put a knot in one corner, and covered it. And he said, whoever is going to pick up the knot, will be the first to jump.

SOPHIA: I always thought it was straws, I always thought it was like a short stick.

ALINA: No, like this, a handkerchief. One of his friends picked up the knot, and they started to file the bars. They opened it. It was a very small opening, like the trains for cows, you know, the cattle cars.

So he is going out and he was scared, and he said he cannot do it, and he came back. So I remember my husband, the first thing he said is, okay, I am going to do it. He pushed him away, and he went out.

And he said—we were changing in the train—and he said, put something warm, like I have high boots and pants, and he looked at me and said, okay. And he went out, and then he comes back.

And he wants to go after him, his friend, and he pushed him away. He said, give me my wife first.

So they picked me up, and he held himself with one hand on the wagon and with the other he took me from the hole, and he took me like this, and we were standing together but between the two wagons. You understand how was that? Between the two cars. Do you have a problem to understand me?

April 23, 1993
U.S. Holocaust Memorial Museum
Washington DC

ALINA: I don't remember if I came first with the feet or with the head.

SOPHIA: Ma, I didn't hear how you started to tell George. How did you do it again? How did you actually . . . how did daddy . . .

GEORGE: Dad filed through the bars.

ALINA: Daddy was first who wants to go, because he was afraid, the other guy . . . He was, daddy, here with the hand, holding here, and the other hand he hold here, someplace. And he pushes me . . . and he holds me and then . . . he holds me like this and pulls me someplace, I don't know where. And I was holding here, and this hand, daddy holds my hand, and daddy's hand was by the second car . . .

SOPHIA: There were two cars connected . . .

ALINA: Two cars connected, trains, not trains, wagons, cars. And that's what we were . . . I think was the . . . you know, the connection. This is the connection. I think we were on this connection.

GEORGE: Yes, that's where it would connect.

ALINA: See, that's on this connection, and daddy was holding the other hand here, I was holding one here, and we jumped.

But I don't remember how, with feet or with my head. With my feet I think I came out.

April 21, 1993
New Haven
Fortunoff Video Archive at Yale

ALINA: Not a window, it wasn't glass. It's just like wires. My husband went, and then he said, give me my wife. His friend wanted to go after him, he said, no, give me my wife. He was something. He was holding himself with one hand. You know, you have a handle on the train. And with the other hand, he took me like this from the opening and pushed down. Then he moved and hold me by one hand, and then said, catch the other. He move and he told me to take it. We were both like this, holding here and holding his hand, and he was teaching me how to jump.

He said, jump in the same direction the train is going, and jump far away. We were talking and he said, are you ready? And I said . . . I don't know . . . I was like ready for everything.

All of a sudden, we saw a light, like a station. That was a station before Treblinka, I think was the name Tluszcz, and he said we had to jump, are you ready?

Tluszcz is located about twenty miles northeast of Warsaw and twenty-five miles southwest of Treblinka.

I said, yes. He pushed me, I fell and I rolled myself to the ditch, and then I hear shooting and shooting because they were on the top of the train.

"One Small Candle," p. 40–41

We stood between the cars balancing ourselves against the sway and pitch of the train. My wife did not know how to fall, and I demonstrated how to hit the ground with her shoulders and roll. I thought she could hear me. I thought she understood. Then I held her, and kissed her, she closed her eyes and I pushed her into the night. Then I made my leap into freedom.

I felt the impact of the roadbed against my shoulders, and I rolled over and over, for the first time I heard shots. I had lost my bread bag in the fall, then more shots and the train was rushing past—but THIS WAS FREEDOM—this was what freedom felt like. [. . .]

Others had jumped after us. All those had been shot. I found their bodies after the train had passed. Further down the track I found my bread bag, and then I walked until I found my wife. She was cut and bruised, but alive. We walked back into the woods and threw up by a stream. Then there was diarrhea. We had seen one man curled up dead in a fetal position. This was all freedom and all storms of war and all nights, and I took off my shirt and ripped it for bandages for the cuts on my wife's arms and side. We waited by the stream, stunned with exhaustion.

ALINA: I was there like in a dream. I didn't know where I am. I didn't know what I have to expect. Nothing. I just hear my voice calling. My husband, he jumped after me, but the train was going so fast that he find himself far away from me. And he was coming slowly and calling, Ala, Ala, Ala.

And I said, yes?

He said, so how you been?

I said, I don't know even.

7

Safe and not safe

April 21, 1993
New Haven
Fortunoff Video Archive at Yale

ALINA: First of all he saved . . . how you call this, what you carry on your back? Knap . . .

DANA: A rucksack.

ALINA: Yes, rucksack. And he put saccharin, bread—a little bread, not too much—soap, tallis, and pictures of family. That was in there. So he have to go back and pick it up and come back, you know, because he throw this first from him. And we start to dig the hole and bury the tallis and the pictures. The rest we took.

And we both went to the woods. From the ditch to the woods. That was a moment, I can't even talk about it.

January 8, 1993
Tamarac

ALINA: He prepared something, you know, he was carrying with him. He took bread, and saccharin, soap, a few things what he got and put in a bag. And pictures from the family, and Jewish Torah, you know? The book to pray.

And when he jumped, he fell down and he was going to look for me. And then I hear he was calling for me, quietly.

How soon I jumped and rolled to the ditch, I hear shooting. So I thought they shoot daddy, you know. I was afraid. But all of a sudden I hear him.

So we were happy and scared both of us, and we went to the woods, and we waited until morning. We were crying. I can't tell you this, we were so scared. We even weren't happy we are alive, that we saved ourselves, you know. It's something, the feeling, you can't say it. We were safe and not safe. We weren't safer than before.

SOPHIA: Didn't they shoot everybody who jumped after you, the friends?

ALINA: They jumped, we found out the next day when my husband went to look for a place for us.

Here, Alina does not mention a tallis, nor that they buried their family pictures by the train tracks. I asked her once if they had tried to recover the buried parcel, but she said it was out of the question.

[34]

First of all, in the morning he left me in the woods and he looked around and he saw a man cleaning, a farmer sweeping his driveway. And he went to him and he made like he was a Polack, you know, praying something, like Gentiles, saying some prayer in the morning. You know, they used to close the stations and take the Poles, and they used to send them to Germany to work—not to get killed, but to work. So he said that he was in the train going to Germany, and he jumped from the train with me.

So he [the farmer] said, call your wife to come here.

He called me. The only thing what I was afraid that then we going to be in trouble because of me, because I looked like a Jew. So I was afraid. So I went over there and he gave us a place to stay, where they kept hay in the . . .

SOPHIA: Barn?

ALINA: Barn. We were there. And I said, listen, he was so nice to us, but you are going to see. We will have to run from here because he will send the Nazis here.

But he was so nice, the Pole was so nice. And he brought us borscht with potatoes. And he apologized that his wife didn't bake him bread today.

And I said, you know what? It makes no sense to be here, because of the neighbors and everything.

April 21, 1993
New Haven
Fortunoff Video Archive at Yale
ALINA: We were afraid to be there too long because the neighbor used to come there. So the only thing what we decide, to start to move to Warsaw, back to Warsaw.

DANA: How did you get back to Warsaw?

ALINA: He was supposed to go and buy the tickets and go over there. My sister was on the Gentile side, and she could help us two, especially me, to come there with somebody, a friend.

But when he went, they closed up the station, the Germans. They were really taking the Poles to go to work to Germany. So I don't know how he managed to come back to me, to the farmer's house, and he said, this is a sign that I shouldn't leave you here, and we are going to move tonight together. Here are the tickets already. He bought the tickets, two tickets. So in the evening we started the trip to Warsaw, by train.

ALINA: He went to buy a ticket, and going there he saw friends killed, you know? They were jumping, and they got killed.

SOPHIA: Everybody.

And we didn't know nothing. We came to Warsaw—I think until eight or nine o'clock you could walk on the streets—and then it was much later. But finally we made it, lucky we made it.

We came to my sister. I don't know how I remember where she was, we went to the wrong house. And then I had to remember her telephone number, and we called her.

And she almost . . . when we came to her house, she fainted. Because my mother, when she came to my house, to our apartment in Warsaw on Yom Kippur, she saw the food on the table, everything was on the table not touched. So she called up my sister and she said, Alinka and Leshek is not alive anymore.

And here I'm coming with my husband. She couldn't believe it.

JARED: And how many sisters did you have?

ALINA: Two. One is alive. I was in the middle, the middle child. I had a sister about one year younger, I remember only one year she was younger because she was only one grade below in school.

SOPHIA: That was Bronka?

ALINA: No, that was Bella.

SOPHIA: . . . I mean Bella.

ALINA: B-E-L- . . .

JARED: Yes. And your other sister?

ALINA: Bronka, Blanche. She's older.

JARED: How much older?

ALINA: I can't put her age. I know, but I can't put because she didn't tell yet anybody, and I don't want to get in trouble.

January 9, 1993
Tamarac

JARED: Were you close to your younger sister?

ALINA: Yes. My younger sister was a beautiful person, very beautiful. She was very talented. I remember that she had a ring, a small ring she got from aunt or from my mother, I don't know. And in ghetto she used to go to special ballet school, but we didn't have money to pay for ballet school, so she sold the ring to go to ballet school.[. . .]

She was a very, very beautiful girl. She managed to go, to be to the Gentile side, until the uprising of the Gentile side. She disappeared. I don't know what happened to her.

JARED: Did you try to find out?

ALINA: Through the Red Cross. My sister [Blanche] told me that she put her over there, in the place, and when she went there, everything was bombed, and the Germans went in, because was uprising, and they bombed the homes, and she was in one of the homes. But I don't know if she ran away or if she was there. Who knows? I don't know how she died.

Circa 1973
Morristown, New Jersey

LEO BACALL: I'm repeating again: just like in concentration camp. You had been scared to death every day because you didn't know when your day's going to come to die in the gas chamber, right? The same was in the Gentile side, that an SS man could come close to you and shoot you in your chest or in your head. So that was the same kind of scariness, but in the ghetto we got used to it. I mean, in the concentration camp, we got used to, we weren't scared anymore. It was always the knowing that someday you're going to die. And someday we'll die anyway, but at this point, this time, it was days . . . count the days you knew you're going to live, but tomorrow might come your number and you got to die. That's it.

March 16, 1994
Tamarac

JARED: Was Leo living with you?

ALINA: No. My husband was my brother-in-law. When he came to me, he was my brother-in-law. And he live in different place because if something happen to me . . .

The Polish uprising in Warsaw began on August 1, 1944, and lasted two months. Fifteen to twenty thousand resistance fighters and 150,000 civilians were killed. After the fall of the city center on October 2, surviving civilians were deported to concentration and labor camps. By the end of the war, 80 percent of Warsaw's buildings had been destroyed and 685,000 of its residents (370,000 of whom were Jews) had been killed.

During the composition of "One Small Candle," around 1972 or 1973, Lawrence Murphy recorded Leo and Alina's stories on cassette, at the Bacalls' home in Morristown, New Jersey. Only a few fragments of these recordings remain in the Bacalls' possession.

JARED: Oh, he pretended to be your brother-in-law?

ALINA: Right. He came to visit and, like, you know . . . and my husband was in Germany, because they were taking Polacks, you know, to Germany, too. And he . . .

JARED: Did you have a different name also? Do you remember?

ALINA: I was Kristina, I think.

JARED: Kristina?

ALINA: Yes. Well, Bakalczuk was the same name, because it's like a Polish name, Russian name.

January 8, 1993
Tamarac

ALINA: I was afraid to go out on the street. I was afraid somebody would find out.

SOPHIA: How old were you then?

ALINA: I was seventeen. It wasn't a life for me there. You know, I said, I miss my parents. Come on, we are going to see my mother and father.

And he said, good, I will see my brother.

Then when we went to the ghetto, they start to clean up the ghetto, *Judenrein.* Daddy bought some things for me so I would look like a Gentile, because they had a different way to dress than the Jews.

He said, you know what? I am going to go out, and then you come out.

And he went out with my things, and the Polacks recognized him. And they said, you're a Jew. And they took everything away from him.

So he came back to the ghetto and he said he felt awful, he felt bad about everything. So we decided to wait, and then we went to my mother and father.

April 21, 1993
New Haven
Fortunoff Video Archive at Yale

ALINA: My mother and father was still in the ghetto. And I said, I miss my mother very much, I would like to go to see her. So we decided to go and we went.

DANA: How were you able to get into the ghetto?

ALINA: We had someone who worked with the underground. A Polish woman, her husband was Jewish and her name was Zosia. She was a beautiful woman. She lost her husband and she had a child

Alina had to invent another husband with Leo standing right beside her.

In fact, when Alina escaped from the Treblinka-bound train, she was already twenty years old.

Judenrein: *cleared of Jews.*

[38]

with him. Even her own child she had to move because the people knew that her husband was Jewish. So what happened, she helped us, she walked with us and we went back to the ghetto. They have something . . . I didn't even ask. She is in Israel now.

We came to my parents, my husband went to his brother to the small ghetto, and then start the terrible . . . they just start again, closing the street. And my mother had prepared . . . you know, they prepared, for my parents . . . had a bunker, a hiding place, but it's just made for so many, so many people . . .

DANA: I have a question to ask. You said you missed your mother and you wanted to go see her. When you went in, did you have the notion you would remain there or that you were going just for a visit?

ALINA: No, just for a visit, just to visit. It was quiet, nobody was after me. I was afraid a lot to be on the street. But when that happened . . .

And they closed up the place where my mother was, and she managed to go to the bunker, and my father was with me, and I went just under the bed. And they were knocking all the doors and they were shooting, because they find somebody in the apartment, they . . . for sure they kill. That was not a hiding place. My heart was beating, and I was laying under the . . . my father went to the attic, went under a bunch of sand. And I hear they opening all the doors and homes and shooting. And finally they passed my apartment. They went out.

January 8, 1993
Tamarac
ALINA: Then we went back on the Gentile side. I told you before what happened—they were looking for us. They found out that we are Jews. That was terrible. I can't believe it, I can't express it, you know. You were so tired of running and to be afraid that you wished to die. Where are you going to run? We were tired.

8

The next half of my life

Circa 1973
Morristown
LEO: Until the Gestapo, I told you about . . .
LAWRENCE MURPHY: No, you didn't.
LEO: No?
LAWRENCE: I don't know how . . .
LEO: Until one night the Gestapo called on my wife's address. She was not there, luckily, because she would have been dead.

At the same night, they called at my house where I used to live.

And they told the lady who she worked for as a babysitter, the girl who is working for you, do you know that she is Jewish?

She said, no, I don't know that she is Jewish.
LAWRENCE: How did they find out?
LEO: I don't know. We don't know.

April 21, 1993
New Haven
Fortunoff Video Archive at Yale

ALINA: Not really to the Gestapo. That was *Volksdeutsch*, working for Gestapo. That was the Polish police.

Volksdeutsch: ethnic Germans living outside Germany.

I said, what? Nothing, they are crazy. I made believe nothing bothers me. I went to bed, but I didn't sleep. In the morning, I run out and I call my sister.

My sister said, you know? Your husband had the same thing. We lived separate.

I said, what? He, too?

And I knew that this guy, because we didn't drink with them, you know, they probably smelled we are Jews. That is what happened and we have to run.

And my sister said to me . . . I called my sister, so she said, wait for me.

I said, where to wait? They're going to come.

Don't worry, stay. You take your stuff what you have there, clothes . . .

I said, Blanche, forget about the clothes, they're going to be soon there, watching me. And that is what was.

I was there in the house, and my sister came, and the guy came who worked for police, *Volksdeutsch*. And he asked her, *Kennkarte*. Mine was not real, but hers was real, because somebody died and she got real papers. And he said to my sister, where you got the *Kennkarte*?

And she says, this is my *Kennkarte*, this is my real *Kennkarte*.

And he says, where is your family?

And she says, I have family. Where she was working, she called the owner *aunt*. So she said, I have my aunt here, I have family.

But with me, he wants to arrest me. And she begged him, and she said, what are you going to have from it? She is so young.

I'm small, so I used to look very young. And finally she went down with him, and she took from me a watch and she took the jewelry and gave it to him.

And then we decided to go to ghetto and be with everybody together. Instead to be killed over there, I said, let me see my parents before I am dying.

And we went over there to the ghetto, and then was the Passover coming, holiday, and uprising in Warsaw ghetto.

That's what start the beginning of the next half of my life.

January 8, 1993
Tamarac

ALINA: We went back to the big ghetto, because they liquidate the small ghetto. They send out all the people. And we went over there, and what start, you know . . . That was April, and we find out they going to come and clean up everybody, take us out. So we decide to fight, not to go like cows, to fight. Anyway we dying, right? So at least we kill a lot of them, a lot of Germans.

JARED: When you say "we" decided, who are you talking about?

ALINA: My husband.

JARED: And were you in contact with a larger group in the underground, or the resistance?

ALINA: Yes, a larger group . . . We found out about the resistance when we saw Jews with German uniforms. You know that? And we got scared.

Like, I went to see my mother. My mother was still there, but I had to go to her. You know, it was like a few streets over. And I'm walking through . . . you know, like the buildings in Europe, three-story building attached to another three-story building, or four-story building, and you could go through the attic from one house to the other. So this way we were going to see my parents. They were working over there for the Germans. They used to work by . . . in the factory where they were making brooms. So we went over there and all of a sudden we see Nazis. And they start to say, we are Jews, don't worry. You know?

So that's what we decided to get a hiding place, and we were fighting. We were killing the Germans. We knew they're going to come, and my husband was out. And we had to throw things on the . . .

They came up this one street, Zamenhofa Street, and there were coming a lot, with the tanks, with everything. And when you start to fight with them, what happened, that they were afraid of us. They went back to the Gentile side, and they start to bomb us with the planes.

April 23, 1993
U.S. Holocaust Memorial Museum
Washington DC
ALINA: *Niska, it was there our bunker.*
GEORGE: *On Niska?*
ALINA: *Yes.*

January 9, 1993
Tamarac
ALINA: This time when I came back to see my mother, that's what happened. One day they came, they say that the Germans were coming. And my mother run to the bunker with my sister, and I was with my father out. Remember, I tell you this story?

April 21, 1993
New Haven
Fortunoff Video Archive at Yale
And I hear they opening all the doors and homes and shooting. And finally, they passed my apartment, they went out.

January 9, 1993
Tamarac
ALINA: When that happened the second time, when they were killing us and they find out the bunker, and my mother told her

[Bella], I'm too old, you go. They had exit to go to the Gentile side, through canals . . .

JARED: Underneath?

ALINA: Underneath, yes.

JARED: Through the sewer?

ALINA: Yes, the sewer. And my mother said, you go, you young, you going to make it.

And they came out because they said they're going to put in gas inside. And they came to Majdanek this time. I was in Majdanek already, I was this time in Majdanek.

JARED: They said they were going to put gas where?

ALINA: To the bunkers, the Germans, because they want everybody to come out.

* * *

ALINA: That was in an attic. It was something, I remember, it was something complicated, the hiding place. We hear, my gosh, that they are going around us and listening to us. They were walking and listening to us. And we stopped breathing. And there was a baby and a mother, and the mother was keeping her hand over the baby's mouth.

JARED: How many people were hiding there?

ALINA: I don't know. There was probably twenty people, twenty. One took poison, didn't want to live. Her nerves, she couldn't take it. I remember, my husband took an egg and put the egg in her mouth, and said, quiet, quiet. Because they were listening.

Then we started to smell smoke, like fire. So always, my husband went out with another guy, I don't remember exactly, to see what was going on, and he saw that it's burning.

So he wants we should leave this bunker and go to another building to see. So daddy started to knock the concrete wall, you know, to make a big hole and we should walk through the hole. Meanwhile, how soon the wall was broken, instead the fire from the other room started to come to us.

Everything was burning around us. So we decided, instead to burn ourselves, to go down, let them kill us.

9 Majdanek

April 21, 1993
New Haven
Fortunoff Video Archive at Yale

ALINA: He said to turn to the wall, hands up. And that's it. I said good-bye to my husband. My husband said good-bye. And that's it.

So, we were standing, standing, and they said, this is too easy for you. You have to suffer before we're going to kill you.

They put us on *Umschlagplatz,* that was like a station in Warsaw ghetto. They put us in the trains, and again we were thinking, jumping or not jumping. So, we were tired. So we said, if we're going to Treblinka, we're going to jump. If we're not going to Treblinka, we going to the camp and see what's going on. Because we were very tired.

January 8, 1993
Tamarac

JARED: Do you remember the arrival there?

ALINA: We arrived to Majdanek, and that was a terrible thing. They separate my husband and me, and they took everything what we had. And I came . . .

SOPHIA: Did you come by train to Majdanek?

ALINA: Yes, that's what we came by train. That was always with the same train that's going to be now in the Washington DC museum.

SOPHIA: So this is from the ghetto where they took you . . .

The freight car on display at the U.S. Holocaust Memorial Museum was instead used to transport Jews from Warsaw to Treblinka, but this interview was recorded before the museum had opened.

ALINA: Yes, that's from uprising. Yes. And they sent us to Majdanek, and I came to Majdanek, they took everything, they put everything, left everything. And I remember, I went to . . . they said we was going to take showers and . . . to the building, they put us to a building. And I was crying because that was the first time they separate us, and I even didn't know how they were killing the people. We didn't know how. We knew they were killing us, but how I didn't know.

March 15, 1994
Tamarac

ALINA: From uprising, they took us to Majdanek. And in Majdanek, the first thing, they told us to give up the jewelry what we have, money, everything. I didn't want to give it to them. So I threw it away some other place.

You know, we were walking. And all of a sudden, I found out that they separate me from my husband. Men goes to the men's *Lager* and I go to the other. And I'm sitting there and I'm crying.

Lager: camp.

First time, you know, we are away. We went through so much together, you know. And jumping from a train, and this was after jumping. Jumping from a train together, we suffer so many years to get here.

I don't know where they took him, and I sit and cry.

January 8, 1993
Tamarac

ALINA: When I came there I was crying, so a German soldier was there. And he said, now you have to be naked, okay? Naked, and you have to take off everything. And he took me, my hand, you know, and I was cursing in Polish terrible. And he took my hand and he's telling me, you're going to take showers here, I'm going to show you.

March 15, 1994
Tamarac

ALINA: After concentration camp, for one year I couldn't take warm showers, only cold showers.

* * *

ALINA: And he came to me, and he said to me, why you crying? You know what? I was cursing him in Polish. He didn't understand I was cursing him.

January 8, 1993
Tamarac

ALINA: And he opened the water to show me. And I said, what does this idiot want, why is he showing me the water? That was the way they were killing us. Instead of water was the gas coming out from it. Did you know that? You know that? You didn't know how

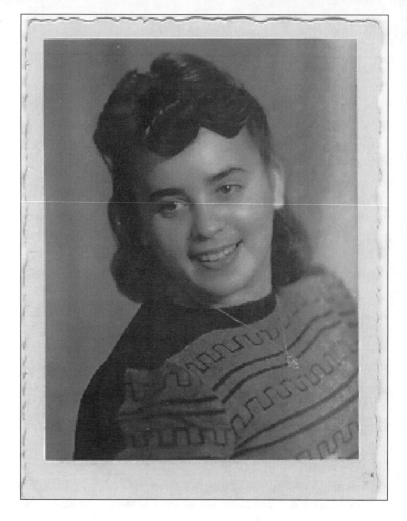

they put the gas through the showers? Instead of water, the gas came and killed the people.

JARED: First he showed you water coming out?

ALINA: He thought I'm crying because I'm going to be dead.

JARED: But he turned on the shower and showed you the water?

ALINA: Yes, he showed me water, and you going to wash. I said to myself what kind of idiot, what is he showing me the water? I know this is water coming. And then, after shower, we have to pass through him, and he was giving us clothes to wear. And I was the only one with a sweater, because he gave me a sweater.

SOPHIA: The same sweater . . . ?

ALINA: I have on the picture even, this sweater.

March 15, 1994
Tamarac

ALINA: And when came, I had to go naked with him, like, you know . . . I was the only one, he handed me sweater. Pink with black . . . stripes . . . hand-made sweater. So I was the only one with sweater in Majdanek.

January 8, 1993
Tamarac

SOPHIA: Was this your sweater or just some other sweater?

ALINA: No, he had bunch of clothes, from other somebody, before us, and he gave me a sweater. And Majdanek was in Poland, and the weather was terrible. It was windy, it was cold and the sweater helped me. But because of the sweater I got so much beaten up you wouldn't believe it, they beat me up.

March 19, 1994
Tamarac

ALINA: And beating every day, every day beating. My body was blue from beating. And I was beginning of pregnancy because this is the beginning in concentration. I didn't know and I didn't eat nothing. And I got twenty-one once, twenty-one times beating.

JARED: When was that?

ALINA: In Majdanek.

JARED: Do you remember the circumstances?

ALINA: Yes.

JARED: What were they?

ALINA: With my friend, and she came sick, I think she's . . . I don't remember exactly, but I think she was pregnant. And in uprising she got rid of the baby because she didn't want to have the baby, you know, in these circumstances. Not pregnant. So when we came to Majdanek, she was sick. She had temperature. But that was . . . they pick up, you know, from our people to watch us, you know, to pick up to work.

January 8, 1993
Tamarac

ALINA: So what you had to do, they made you carry stones from one side to the other. You know, to walk, to put the stone over there and then to pick up the stone and put back there. Or to a big hole. You know, heavy, heavy, very heavy work. And the girl who was taking care of us was a terrible, terrible woman, and she wants to take her to work. And I said, don't take her. I will go to work for her, she is sick.

April 21, 1993
New Haven
Fortunoff Video Archive at Yale
ALINA: I was afraid of beatings because I didn't want to be crippled. I said to myself, if something, then let them shoot me, to finish my life, because it was very hard to live, very hard. Many times I was thinking to go on the wire, where you touch it and just finish my life.

And in the back of my head was, who would tell the world what happened? Always the same thing.

January 8, 1993
Tamarac
ALINA: People were dying, they wanted to die, they went on the electric wires in a place. And they put electric wires what you touched it, you got killed.

April 21, 1993
New Haven
Fortunoff Video Archive at Yale
ALINA: You know, in Majdanek was a terrible camp. They were telling us to take off our shoes, you know, shoes, boots . . . And they were telling us to walk on the small stones, to go to a certain point. They said, go there and pick up a stone and bring on this side.

I walk, and I am telling you that was suffering to go on this.

And I pick up a stone and I couldn't pick up, so I tried to pick up the small one, and then I got beaten. We all, not only me, everyone in Majdanek got beaten up.

Syzyfowe prace: *a Sisyphean task.* You know, we call that *Syzyfowe prace.* You know what that means? That means that just to torture, just to let us suffer, because what's the difference? Take out the stone from this side and bring on this. And then from this side, to bring back there.

January 8, 1993
Tamarac
ALINA: So she pushed me away. I don't want you, I want her.

So I pushed her back, I thought I'm still at home. So she hit me. I hit her back.

So she went to the German Nazi and said someone beat her up.

So she [the Nazi] said, who?

So she said, somebody wearing a sweater with pink and black.

The Nazi was looking after me and all of a sudden she told me to lie down on the bench and twenty times she beat me with a leather strap.

* * *

But because of the sweater I got so much beaten up you wouldn't believe it.

March 19, 1994
Tamarac
JARED: A whip?

ALINA: A whip, and she hit me twenty-one. I couldn't walk. And three months later, I went to Auschwitz. I still . . . when I can't walk, everybody ask me, what you have hurts up there?

I said, not so fun, I said.

I'm done with story. This story, that's what I remember.

10 Auschwitz-Birkenau

January 8, 1993
Tamarac

ALINA: One day, three months later, I said to myself, the next transport I am going to volunteer. So I volunteered and they sent us to Birkenau.

July 11, 1994
West Hartford

ALINA: It was a big tragedy in Majdanek because you close to your family, you find out every day they're dying, they're killed, you know.

If you go to Auschwitz, you don't know anybody anymore, you know. You busy with yourself. That's what happened.

March 16, 1994
Tamarac

ALINA: And my father was in Majdanek, and she ask . . . and he asked me where my mother, and I told that she's working. I didn't want to tell him that, you know, she's dead.

JARED: So you saw your father?

ALINA: What?

JARED: You saw your father?

ALINA: I saw my father. But my father have condition. You know, diabetes he was. And he used to take three times a day insulin so he didn't have to swell up. His kidney went, I think. He swell up. So they put him on, like, *Revier*. You know what is *Revier*? Like a hospital. Make-believe. They give him needle to sleep. They killed him.

Revier: *infirmary.*

JARED: Do you remember how you got to see him?

ALINA: Yes. Through the fence. Here was for women camp, and here was like the transport camp, right? So they put the men different place than the women, but close to each other.

JARED: And the train was on the tracks?

ALINA: Only . . . no train, no train. Only a fence, not a wood fence, you know, an iron fence was separating us. And through this we see each other.

January 8, 1993
Tamarac

JARED: When you left Majdanek, you could volunteer? They would ask for volunteers?

ALINA: No, you just see that they are picking up for transport and you just run to the line and wait.

JARED: Where was your husband then?

ALINA: Still there. We were going to Birkenau, and before going on the train they gave us coffee. Coffee? Ha! It was more like mud. And somebody was sitting and giving me the coffee and I wanted to take the cup and I couldn't, because the guy kept it back. And I looked, and it was my husband.

SOPHIA: On the train?

ALINA: No, not on the train, before going to the train, because he was working in the kitchen and he knew that the next transport, that on the next transport I was going to Auschwitz. So he went to give us coffee, you know. He said, don't worry, the next transport I am going to be there, I'm going.

April 21, 1993
New Haven
Fortunoff Video Archive at Yale

ALINA: He was working in the kitchen, and they sent him to give us tea before we step to the train. And I grab the tea and I see somebody hold the cup and I look and it's my husband. He said, don't worry, I am going to follow.

* * *

ALINA: I said to myself, the first transport they going to move from Majdanek, I am going to go. And that was maybe three months after being in Majdanek.

We took the transport and we went to Auschwitz, to Birkenau. They took us to Birkenau. And they took us there, and the first thing, they were taking hair off from all your body. Everything, wherever you have hair. And men was doing that. And we were all young girls, and that was terrible things.

January 8, 1993
Tamarac

ALINA: I came there to Auschwitz-Birkenau and I looked around, and it was burning, the chimneys were smoke, smoke was coming from the chimneys.

I asked one Polish girl what that was.

She said, the girl, a bakery. They are baking bread.

I said, what are you talking about? I didn't understand that they were burning people. I knew they were killing but I still didn't know how they were killing them.

And so the first thing, they were cleaning us, taking hair, you know, shaving our hair. The men were shaving us, even on the bottom, all over. Men, not women. This was a terrible experience.

They gave me a number, the number, a tattoo. And then they sent you to the camp to work. And I worked in the woods. Digging graves. I don't even know, they didn't put us in the graves, but I don't know for what we're doing that.

March 16, 1994
Tamarac

ALINA: I didn't know that they going to shave our head. So all over. And men were doing that. Terrible, was terrible.

Before that start, we felt like nobody. And they letting some people, you know, could . . . they were Jews. Jewish men they do that. They pick up men to do that. And they were heartbroken.

JARED: Do you remember the man who cut your hair?

ALINA: No. I don't look at his face, you know. I was shy, and I was . . . I feel, like, terrible, like a piece of *shmate*, you know? Like a piece of rag. First of all, when they shave my hair, you know, my hair, I wasn't upset about it. Because I remember my friend start to cry.

JARED: What color was your hair?

ALINA: Black.

JARED: It wasn't bleached anymore?

ALINA: Oh, no. Was bleached, right. You're right, was bleached. My hair was already growing black, you know. But was light, light. Not black like I was born.

* * *

ALINA: Yes. My hair was blond.

JARED: You dyed your hair?

ALINA: Not me, but somebody, you know, who help me to go there. A friend of my sister . . . she make . . . she bleach my hair. And . . .

JARED: Blonde?

This took place on the Gentile side of Warsaw, before Alina returned to the ghetto and was sent to Majdanek.

ALINA: With my eyes, black eyes, and my complexion was . . . I was different than anybody else. I was afraid everybody's looking at me, that they recognize me.

April 21, 1993
New Haven
Fortunoff Video Archive at Yale

ALINA: All of a sudden, I see my friend. I look at her and she looks at me, and she cry about her hair.

I look at her, and mirrors we don't have, but in a window I look at myself, and I start to laugh hysterical.

And I said, you crying about your hair? You are not going to live here too long, I said. You're not worried you are going to die? You're crying about your hair, you lost your hair?

March 18, 1994
Tamarac

ALINA: I don't know. He fall from the steps and he looked so funny.

He said, you're laughing and I am hurt. I couldn't stop laughing. I started to help him but I was still laughing.

Isn't that crazy? Sometimes you just can't help it. Did you have this feeling sometime, like playing ball and the guy falls and looks so funny and you start to laugh about it, and then you find out he is hurt very badly? I felt so bad. He was so angry at me.

He said, what are you laughing at? I am hurt.

Alina recalls an incident that took place after she and Leo had moved to the United States.

March 16, 1994
Tamarac

ALINA: And, you know, in the window I look at myself and I start to laugh hysterical. I start to laugh how I look without hair. She was crying, I was laughing. I will never forget.

JARED: There was a mirror that you looked in?

ALINA: No mirror. A window. In the glass, sometimes you could see yourself, right?

* * *

ALINA: And then there was a line, everybody. Shave, shower, number, clothes.

* * *

ALINA: And she look at me, and she was nice to me because was a small number. Some girls have big numbers. And she said, this is a bakery. And I believed it was a bakery.

JARED: And you were . . . she was standing up, also? Or she was sitting down?

ALINA: No, she was sitting at a small table. Something, you know, like . . . and she had the needle. And she was making the number on me. And she said, like this, I should be strong, you know.

JARED: And you were standing up?

ALINA: Yes.

* * *

ALINA: There was, like . . . a triangle. See, right here. That mean I'm a Jew.

JARED: Then where was the number?

ALINA: The number was here. Forty-six. What is that? Forty-six? Forty-six, seven, I think. Four, seven, six. Okay. Four-seven-six.

You know, I don't remember. Four . . . and what is that? Ninety. See that, I'm block completely on the number.

It was like this, and this in the center. It's still very little here. And . . .

JARED: Which way were the numbers facing?

ALINA: To you.

JARED: To me?

ALINA: Yes. To you.

* * *

JARED: When did you get the tattoo? When did you get the number?

ALINA: Over there. The same time. Shaving, the clothes, and number they giving you.

JARED: How did they give you a number?

ALINA: How? With needle. They pinch like, you know, with ink and goes in. This is what . . . this is way to carve this, isn't it? But this is not like a plastic operation, just . . .

The doctor who did operation on me . . . They beat me . . . I had . . . I don't know if you know about it. You know the story?

JARED: I think so.

ALINA: When the doctor operate me?

JARED: Here in the States?

ALINA: Right.

JARED: Why did he operate on you?

ALINA: From the beating. When I got the twenty-five on my back, I got a blood clot. And when I came here, I didn't do nothing about it. But when they start talking about cancer, I went to doctor. And that's what he said to me that he's worried because it's blocked. So he wants to take out the number, too. He did it. He said, I don't charge you.

JARED: Did you want to have the number removed?

ALINA: No. But I remember when the people ask me what the number is on the train. And I got annoyed. I was angry that the people don't know what this is, you know.

And I came home and I said, you know, to my husband, doctor wants to take out the number. He don't want to charge.

He said, but I need memory, to remember.

I said, I will remember anyway, even I don't have a number.

And my husband say, you know what? I will kill you if you going to do that.

He didn't want me to do it.

April 23, 1993
Washington DC

ALINA: I wasn't born with that. Why I have to have that? They forced to put some number here. I wasn't ashamed. And you know, the doctor wants to take out, he told us I'm going to forget about things what happened to me.

[55]

And I said, you never can forget things what I went through. It's only going to stay in my head.

March 15, 1994
Tamarac
JARED: *Do you remember the number you had on your arm?*
ALINA: *I don't remember . . . forty-nine, I remember. I have it on citizen papers.*
JARED: *But you don't remember the whole thing?*
ALINA: *I probably don't want to know.*

United States of America
Certificate of Naturalization
No. 7380610
Tattoo left arm - 476490

* * *

ALINA: And that was a terrible operation on the blood clot what I have. And he went . . . he didn't realize it's so deep. I felt the knife, you know, how they cut. I said, doc, I feel everything. So he give me a little more anaesthetic.

JARED: And what did Leo say when you came home without a number?

ALINA: He didn't . . . he didn't say nothing. That's what I want, you know. He said, I'm stupid. I remember. I don't want to . . .

JARED: What did your children say?

ALINA: My children right away? Nothing. They didn't say nothing. Georgie was six years old, and he was making breakfast for me.

A connection

11

April 21, 1993
New Haven
Fortunoff Video Archive at Yale
ALINA: And they took us to the barracks and we were sitting for a while. Then they move us in other place. And I remember I work with the Kommando, it's number 103, I think, or 102. I am not sure. The same thing. In the woods, digging.

And I remember I got very sick, very sick. And they said, don't go, they call it hospital, *Revier*. They said, don't go to hospital, don't go to hospital.

I said, what kind of hospital? I cannot work. I had forty-two temperature, forty-two. I was collapsing, and I said, I don't care, let them take me to crematorium. I can't work, I can't work. So finally, they took the temperature, I had forty, so they sent me to work.

But then when I had forty-two and I was already unconscious, so they sent me to the little hospital. And I had the typhus. I went through typhus.

January 8, 1993
Tamarac
ALINA: I couldn't walk. I had a high temperature, and I knew if I go to the hospital—like a hospital, but it wasn't hospital, just a barracks, with a few girls—they beat you up, that's it. I knew if I went there they would put me straight to the crematorium. But I wasn't able to walk anymore. I had a high temperature.

When I came there, I didn't remember, but I was out of order, I was like unconscious.

All of a sudden, after twelve days . . . they were saying if you wake up after ten or twelve days after having typhus and you are alive, you will make it.

I didn't know I had typhus, I knew that I had a high temperature, and I didn't know what was going on with me.

You know the tragedy? They put me with a girl from Greece, in the same little bed, like a bed. And she had the sickness what you scratch all the time, you get it from the woods . . .

SOPHIA: Poison ivy? Poison oak?

ALINA: Something like this. I got that from her too.

After twelve days, they tell me, I opened my eyes and I was screaming that she stole my bread. You know when you were hungry, you dream about bread, it is on your mind. She run to me, the woman who was taking care, and she picked up the small pillow and saw so much bread was over there, so she start to beat me up. I said she ate my bread up, and here is my bread. You know, twelve days' daily portion of bread. For twelve days I didn't eat it so it was under my pillow.

When I asked her what happened to me, she said, you have typhus.

And I said, give me something to drink. I was burning inside. So she gave me water to wash myself. I took the whole thing and I drank it. So I got beaten again.

You are not a person, you are nobody there. They don't respect you. You know I did that because I was burning from the fever, maybe that is what kept me alive, the water I drank. For twelve days I didn't drink nothing.

Finally, after that, when I came to myself, I used to sew aprons for the girls what were taking care of us, and they would give me something to eat. They give you soup, or a little bit more bread. I was very handy with sewing.

Then came a time that they sent me from the block to go to work, and I went to work. I remember, 103rd Kommando. They sent me back to the woods to work again.

March 16, 1994
Tamarac

ALINA: If you get up, you're alive. That's what happened to me. After ten days I was unconscious.

January 8, 1993
Tamarac

JARED: So every morning you would leave the camp to go into the woods?

ALINA: Yes. We went there, and we came back from a whole day and they gave us water with sand and grass. And that was the food.

* * *

SOPHIA: Did daddy come back for you?

ALINA: I found out daddy when I left the hospital. You know, like a hospital, they called it that. I didn't know about daddy. I find out after a week or two that my husband is alive. We had a connection because he sent letters through the guy and he told me when he came to Auschwitz and to Birkenau.

April 21, 1993
New Haven
Fortunoff Video Archive at Yale
ALINA: Then I find out . . . when I came after typhus, they sent me to camp where they going to send us to work.

And I look out, and I saw men working on the roof, first time. So I called one guy, and I said, maybe you know someone by the name of Bakalczuk?

He said, Bakalczuk, sure, he has it good here.

I said, what do you mean "good"?

January 8, 1993
Tamarac
ALINA: A guy, you know, who was taking care of the Jewish men and people from prison. They clean up the prison, murderers. And they were taking care of daddy and other people.

He saw my husband and he ask him if he knows German, how to write and read.

He said, yes, I know.

He took him in and he was telling him to write how much stuff is going out from the camp for the guys who repaired the roofs. That's why I got the contact with him, through this guy.

April 21, 1993
New Haven
Fortunoff Video Archive at Yale
ALINA: He told me, he has a good job. I'm working on the roof and he marks down how many nails is going out, you know, like an accountant for the Kapo.

And I said, okay, you going to take a few words for my husband?

I was so happy I found him, because he told me, next transport I will follow you. But we weren't sure when.

Kapo: from Italian, capo (head). Non-Jewish prisoners in charge of a block or barracks.

January 8, 1993
Tamarac

ALINA: And he was writing to me that he had it good with him because he can help him with food, but when he gets drunk he beats him up, he broke his ribs.

SOPHIA: He broke daddy's ribs?

ALINA: Yes, he beat him up and only because he could help me, he stayed.

April 21, 1993
New Haven
Fortunoff Video Archive at Yale

ALINA: He said, if you give me soup I will give him the letter. You know, a little soup.

I was so hungry but I managed to have two spoons and I gave it to him. Next day he is coming, and I said, so?

He said, I gave him the letter.

So I figured, oh, he is lying probably.

But all of a sudden, you know, my husband came to the barracks.

Selection

12

January 9, 1993
Tamarac

ALINA: I'm a little, you know, a little angry what I went through. Why I have to be a young girl, not to have my young years' experience. I was taken out from school. I married very young and I even don't know why I married. I was very inexperienced.

And in Europe, a girl seventeen is like here a girl ten. We don't talk about sex, you don't know nothing about sex, you don't know how to have a baby even.

When I took . . . my oldest sister was allowed to take books in library and she have a book about sex, and I took the book. And my mother saw me reading, she took away from me. And I probably will not understand anything what is in the book.

So when I was pregnant, I even didn't know . . . I knew how the baby comes. But what I should expect, nothing. And so for four months or five months, I don't know how long, I didn't know that I'm pregnant.

All of sudden to find out, and so I was sure, that's it. Next, I will go. And I'm still alive, and I made it. And I'm happy I made it.

March 15, 1994
Tamarac

ALINA: So I was thinking about it. The whole nine months what I was pregnant, about the time what I had with my husband. The good time, I mean.

January 8, 1993
Tamarac

SOPHIA: Mom, explain that story to Jared, when daddy came and said you looked pregnant.

ALINA: I told you in the car. When he came, he said, you know, you look like pregnant. My husband, when he came to see me.

JARED: When he came to see you in the hospital?

ALINA: No.

JARED: When he came to see you at the barracks before you went to the hospital?

ALINA: Yes, when I sent with the guy a little soup and told him that I . . .

SOPHIA: You didn't tell Jared this, Ma. You told Charlie and me this afternoon. So he doesn't know this story.

ALINA: So that's the story. It's that this was the guy who was fixing the roof, I gave him the soup, and he went to my husband and told him that . . . I told you this story . . .

SOPHIA: No, you never finished it.

ALINA: I'm here, and I hear that he's there, and they're calling me, and I got up from the bunk and I saw my husband.

So, my husband wants to kiss me. I said, don't kiss me, look at the children, they are burning people here and everything.

And all of a sudden he said, I brought you some food. And he told me about his job and how he got his job.

April 21, 1993
New Haven
Fortunoff Video Archive at Yale

ALINA: He told me this story. He works for a Kapo, and he has enough food and he will be able to help me. But he's such a murderer that when he is drunk, he broke my three ribs, he said. He is beating me up and I want to leave him. But now that I find you, I will probably stay, because I could help you.

January 8, 1993
Tamarac

ALINA: When I came back, I said to the girls, you know, my husband told me I look like pregnant.

And they said, yes, you do look like you're pregnant.

I said, what? So I said, how I will find out if I am pregnant? Because we didn't get our periods there.

So one of the girls said, you know, when my sister was pregnant . . . and we start to figure out how many months, from the Warsaw uprising, Majdanek, and Auschwitz. Was maybe together three months or four months.

And she said, try your breasts, see if you have milk, she had milk.

That is how I found out I was pregnant. Then I was running from everybody.

evening of January 9, 1993
Tamarac
Running before my eyes. Can I say that? Running before my eyes.

January 8, 1993
Tamarac
ALINA: They were telling pregnant women they would get white bread and good food. And I didn't trust them and didn't go, and I begged the other girls not to go. They are killing our parents, they are killing us, and you believe they care about the pregnant women?

But hunger is terrible. For a piece of bread they didn't think about it.

That's when I found out I was pregnant.

March 15, 1994
Tamarac
JARED: At that point how many months pregnant were you? Do you know?

ALINA: I don't know. Three months, maybe four months. I found out late. I didn't know, because nobody got their periods out there. As soon as they stopped giving you food, you didn't have your monthly thing. And I find out I was already having milk in my breasts. It must be fifth month.

April 21, 1993
New Haven
Fortunoff Video Archive at Yale
ALINA: And I squeezed my breast and I saw milk coming. Then I realized that I'm pregnant. And that's my other suffering. To hide, to run away from everything.

I remember was selection. And I went to the selection. They select for left and right.

And I came there naked, and he looked at me and said, *bis du schwanger*? That means, are you pregnant?

And the same minute a guy, another soldier on a motorcycle, came to him.

And everybody say, go, go.

So I run past, I went to the right side.

And, miracles. Every time I am alive, that's just miracles happen.

13 Only me

April 21, 1993
New Haven
Fortunoff Video Archive at Yale

DANA: Is there anything else you would like to add? You have told us a lot this morning.

ALINA: I want to add about my husband, who is not alive. He is the biggest hero. I live because of him.

When I was pregnant, in Auschwitz, in Birkenau, they sent me to dead barracks—from over there, they putting in crematoriums—because they couldn't keep me on the block.

And I asked the *Blockälteste* if she would just let me say good-bye to my husband, and she said, okay, but have to be very fast.

January 8, 1993
Tamarac

ALINA: Do you know what the *Blockälteste* is? This was somebody that took care of us in the barracks, and she was a Polish girl and she was taking care of all the girls, and she watched us so we would go to work and clean the barracks. She was a nice girl because she got from my husband food. He said, watch her.

April 21, 1993
New Haven
Fortunoff Video Archive at Yale

ALINA: So I wrote a letter to the same guy, what I mentioned before, and I told my husband in the letter that they taking me. And I said good-bye to him, and I explained, I tell him everything, you know. To live and to be strong, to tell the world what happened.

March 15, 1994
Tamarac

ALINA: A good-bye letter, I thought. And my husband wrote me a beautiful letter, and I realize that he's right. He said, how about me? You know, you have to live for me. If you want me to live, you have to live for me. You know, a beautiful letter he sent me and . . . and I realize I, you know, I have to be stronger. Help me, the letter help me a lot. Well, that was . . .

JARED: What happened to the letter?

ALINA: What?

JARED: Do you know what happened to the letter?

ALINA: What? We don't have nothing. Whatever I have in concentration camp, I left there. Because they change your clothes, and you don't want to have anything on you because they could beat you up. Especially letters. We didn't save anything.

January 8, 1993
Tamarac

ALINA: I didn't finish my story before. I wrote a letter to my husband that I am going to die, he should come to say good-bye.

Hey, I have to make supper?

SOPHIA: It's enough, Ma.

ALINA: What time is it?

SOPHIA: Twenty after five.

ALINA: It's late.

He came and he went to a German woman.

JARED: Your husband?

ALINA: He kissed her boots and he begged her. She was with a gun, she could take the gun and kill him. He said he didn't have anybody, only me, and please don't let her die.

Who would do that? Not one man from all would go to a German woman for help. He said, if she is going to kill me, she will kill me. Do you know that she saved me? She sent my number to the *Blockälteste* and she said to send me to the hospital and not to the death camp.

Circa 1973
Morristown

ALINA: You know, she could just take out a gun and shoot him. Again, I don't know what happened. She told him, okay, she will stay.

LEO: Was I alone, or was I with Zepel?

ALINA: You was alone, you know, you went on . . . he went on his knees and start to kiss her feet, to let me stay on, not to die. So she got order, my *Blockälteste*, to keep me, not to send me to the dead barracks.

LEO: How did she get the order?

ALINA: From her, from the German *Aufseherin*.

Again, this is from a fragment of tape recorded by Lawrence Murphy while preparing "One Small Candle."

Aufseherin: *female camp guard working for the SS.*

[65]

LEO: From the SS.

ALINA: Yes, from the SS woman. And again I'm still alive, half-dead. You know, how you call? Half-dead.

Again the same. And that was already, I would say, in beginning of my ninth month. She came again to me.

LEO: December 1943.

ALINA: She came to me, the *Blockälteste*, and she said, listen, they going to clean out the camp today. What to do with you? They going to pick you out, and I don't know what to do with you. But instead to send you to dead barracks, I will send you to *Revier*. And maybe over there you will be lucky to . . .

LEO: . . . survive.

ALINA: . . . to survive.

April 21, 1993
New Haven
Fortunoff Video Archive at Yale

ALINA: He helped me through his Kapo. He said, I have a wife here, she is pregnant.

He beat him up that he didn't tell him that. You know, he beat him up, but he came and he helped me. And he went to the *Blockälteste* from one of the barracks where only Gentile people are there, okay? And he said, listen what will happen with her is going to happen the same to you, and you have to save her.

Circa 1973
Morristown

ALINA: I went over there, and again my husband find out that I'm over there. So he wrote me a letter and told me, listen, listen, write a letter, in German, to my Kapo, maybe he could do something. So I wrote him a beautiful letter in German, that he probably has kids and a wife, and he understand me, that I would like to live, and that I'm sure that I'm going to be dead. You know, the whole thing, and he probably, everything . . . I just want him to come, maybe he could help me with something.

So he went to my husband, and he said, why didn't you tell me that you have a wife? Anyway, to make a long story short, he came with a package, butter, and meat, and kielbasa, and salami, sugar, everything . . . He went to me . . .

Anyway, at this time, when I was in *Revier*, was two *Blockältesten*, two sisters from Czechoslovakia, and he just called them and said like this, if anything happen to her, the same thing going to happen to you both.

LAWRENCE: Why was he so friendly with you, Leo?

LEO: Because of my Kapo, because of that Mr. Zepel, who was my Kapo.

ALINA: No, he asked you why he was so good to you.

LEO: Zepel?

LAWRENCE: Yes. There's that story where he kicked you once . . .

ALINA: Yes, and break his two ribs.

LEO: Break my ribs, and then he cried for me, oh what have I done? What have I done? My best boy, I nearly killed him, and so forth.

He was very good to me because he needed me, and he was very happy with me. I was very decent and honest with him, because he left me all his diamonds and gold and everything to trade with the Germans, with the SS, you know?

He said, here's everything, and you've got to talk to them. Whatever they'll bring you, you pay with these things.

And we hid everything, it was in actually covered . . . in one of the ceilings in an unfinished barrack. All I had to do was move one part of the . . . one piece of the wooden board, and move it aside, and I had everything, all counted, and everything was laying there, and that was all for my Kapo, okay? Whatever I had done, any tradings throughout the day, I gave him the report at night, that I got this for this, and this for that. And he said, okay. He called me *Schreiber*, you know, because I used to take care of the stock.

Schreiber: writer.

March 16, 1994

Tamarac

ALINA: The *Blockälteste*, who Zepel talked to her, she said, you know what, you're going to pass selection, you couldn't see the stomach. You know?

So when she said that to me, I said, oh my gosh, I'm going to be dead in few hours.

They find out that next day's going to be selection. So in middle of night she wasn't quite sure. She came. She put a white sheet on me, and she said, come on with me.

And I went with her and she put me in barracks where the Gentile people are allowed to have babies, and the *Blockälteste* was a Yugoslavian Gentile. And she was hiding me there.

Like, the German walk in, and they ask her, do you have Jews here?

And she said, no.

That was beautiful from her because if they will find . . . look only on the number, because we have on the number like a piece of star. You know, that means you are Jewish. So if they came and look at me, and on the number, they will know that I'm a Jew.

January 8, 1993
Tamarac

ALINA: So I hear that when they took us to the crematorium, we

"Hatikva" (Hope): song adopted as the official Zionist anthem in 1933. Now Israel's national anthem.

were singing "Hatikva" before we went, because we knew we were going to die. So everybody was singing "Hatikva," and I knew they were making the hospital clean. And all of a sudden the Germans came to the barracks where I was with the Yugoslavian *Blockälteste* and they asked, do you have Jews here?

And she said, no.

I heard that. My heart was beating so hard, and that was beautiful because she risked her own life. If they would go and look on the hand, because we used to have, the Jews used to have like a half star on the hand, they would know I was Jewish. She really took a chance.

And I stayed alive, and I had my baby. But this is for another time.

On the oven

March 16, 1994
Tamarac

ALINA: I was here with her only. I remember only her. I don't
know why, but I remember her. I didn't see any other people there.

JARED: Where was she from?

ALINA: From Russia. And I ask her . . . I was still pregnant. She
told me she gave birth to a dead baby.

And I ask her, if I have a baby, she will be able to take care of the
baby? And then after the war, when the wars end, and I told her . . .
I promised her everything.

And she said I should understand her, that it's very hard even for
her to have a baby.

I understand.

To go to work, who going to take care of the baby? And she said,
it's too hard.

And I was talking Polish to her, because I couldn't talk Russian to
her. I know words, but I didn't speak to her.

January 9, 1993
Tamarac

ALINA: So, I remember the next day she was telling me, you know,
you didn't tell me you talk Russian, you were talking to me in your
dream, Russian. And you speak beautifully in Russian.

I never speak beautifully in Russian, you know. I couldn't understand how I was talking to her conversation in Russian language. I
never went to school to learn Russian. Only what I hear from my
mother.

* * *

ALINA: My mother, she speak Russian. She used to sing Russian
songs. She used to talk to us Polish. But we understood Russian, too.

March 16, 1994
Tamarac
JARED: Did she tell you what you said?

ALINA: Yes.

JARED: What did you say?

ALINA: That I talk about baby what going to be born. She should take care, you know. And I will pay for that later on when we going to be free. And like, you know, like . . . that's what I was talking with her. I talk Russian.

And I said, I don't know. I was . . . until today, I don't understand how I was talking Russian. I don't know. And that was terrible time. I was, you know . . . that was in February I have the baby. I think twenty-one or twenty-two. That's the number what stay in my mind.

But all the time when I was there, I don't know how long, the baby was pushing on me, you know. And I have to go very often to the toilet.

Alina seems to associate the day of the baby's birth with her own birthday, February 5, 1922.

March 19, 1994
Tamarac
ALINA: I figured out, I don't remember, but I figured out I gave birth to my child, my baby, in December.

January 9, 1993
Tamarac
ALINA: *Only what I hear from my mother.* And I said, I don't know. Maybe only in dream, my dreams.

And I was thinking, you know, every time I remember. Some things, you know, stay in my memory.

April 21, 1993
New Haven
Fortunoff Video Archive at Yale
ALINA: In the beginning I didn't know that I'm pregnant. But when I find out, that was hard to understand what I went through. Especially, the last days when the child was pushing to go out and I was afraid I'm going to make on the, how do you call, the beds, you know, the bunkbeds, and they going to beat me up.

And I was so afraid because I got twenty-one in Majdanek. And all the time my body was, you know, blue. My whole body was blue.

* * *

ALINA: That was in December, and, I would say, a mile to go to the toilets outside, without shoes. I was walking, running, and when I came back, I couldn't go to bed because I need again to go. So all night, the last months, I was going, in snow. That's a torture.

January 9, 1993
Tamarac
SOPHIA: What about the toilets?
ALINA: The toilets? It was like, outside . . .
SOPHIA: Like an outhouse?
ALINA: What outhouse?
SOPHIA: Like an outhouse, they call them outhouses now, here, when you have a toilet outside, like when you're at a fair and you go outside to the toilet.
ALINA: It was like toilet, and there was sitting here, and sitting here. Everybody together. I was afraid that I was going to make in bed, so I went to the toilet, and then went home to the barracks, and before I went to lie down I went again, because I was running all the time in the snow, that was . . . Nobody went through what I went through. And I stayed alive, and I'm here.
SOPHIA: My hero, my mommy. I love you mommy . . . So are you going to come for Pesach, and spend Pesach with us, because you hate the holidays and you want to be near your children?
ALINA: I hate the holidays, I don't want to be with nobody for the holidays. I hate them.

March 16, 1994
Tamarac
ALINA: And the toilets was outside. You know, like, further than this building. You know, over there, you see the building? More though.

Alina gestures toward her neighbor's house.

JARED: So fifty or sixty feet away?
ALINA: I don't know. Probably. For me it was long. When I came over there, and went home in snow without shoes, running . . .

When I came to the bed, I had to get up again. So the whole night I was running back there. All night. That was my pregnancy.

And all of a sudden one day . . . I lost the water. That's what you want you hear about? And I was on my . . . I didn't know that the water break, you know? I thought that I make in bed. And I was crying that they going to beat me up. And I start to . . . I didn't scream, but

[71]

just for making . . . like that the woman who was there and knew how to deliver the baby . . . she was . . . how you can say?

JARED: Midwife?

ALINA: Midwife. And she came to me and she said, come, come, come you going to have a baby. Come on the oven. It was a big . . . you know, for the barracks. Bricks, made from bricks. And on the each side was a door, metal door. And the fire, like a fireplace, from one side to the other. Some people put pot with food to cook there, you know. Who cook a lot, cook a lot. And I remember I was there . . .

April 21, 1993
New Haven
Fortunoff Video Archive at Yale

ALINA: And when I came back one time from the outside, I got terrible pains. And we have a midwife in the barracks, and she hear the way, you know . . . And she said to me, come on the oven. You know, in the barrack was a brick oven going through. Come on the oven. I went on the oven, and the baby was born.

I still hear the cry

15

March 16, 1994
Tamarac

JARED: Do you remember what you were thinking?

ALINA: What?

JARED: Do you remember what you were thinking? What you were feeling?

ALINA: What I was feeling? Pain. And I just was thinking about my husband. My husband was sick. I didn't know if he was having typhus. In the same time I find out. And my sister-in-law die, from pneumonia, I think. And I'm giving birth to my child, and I have to go with the child to crematorium. Because that's what . . . I didn't think about to live.

And I think, I couldn't save the baby. And I'm giving the baby . . . I give birth to the baby to be killed. And I didn't have time to be too much in pain, because the baby was born in one second. And normal. I didn't rip anything inside because it was normal birth.

JARED: And the midwife assisted you?

ALINA: Yes. She pick up the baby, and I only ask her, what is it? She said, it's a boy.

And I went to the bed and I said, I wish my husband were with me. And then I thought she going to clean up the baby and give me to my bed, to feed the baby. I hear the baby crying and crying and crying. And one day, and second day . . .

And I said to her, give me my baby. I want to feed him, feed the baby.

And she came to my bed and she start to talk to me and she said . . . I said, where is the baby?

She said, it's in the, in the . . . you know, the sick people, some go there, too. Sick people.

JARED: Yes.

ALINA: And she put the baby into the sick person *Revier* and wait until the baby die. Because she was religious person, very religious, too. And she will not kill the baby. She will not do anything wrong.

And I hear the baby crying. And I said, give me the baby. I'm going to . . .

And she said, if I give you the baby, you're going with the baby. You know what I mean?

I said, that's what I want. I want to go. I'm tired already. And I want to go with the baby to the crematorium. I want to die with my baby.

And she said to me, you're young. You going to see your husband. I remember the words what she said. You're young, you going to have more children. You know?

And I said, I want my baby, and I cry. And I scream, give me my baby, give me my baby. And I cry.

Maybe a week the baby was alive, because I hear the crying. Maybe five days, maybe six days, the baby was crying.

And I want the baby, and I still hear the cry.

April 21, 1993
New Haven
Fortunoff Video Archive at Yale
ALINA: She said, you have a boy. And she took away the boy, and until today I don't know where is the boy.

I beg her, I hear crying, and I ask her to give me the baby. I'm very . . . I said, I don't want to live. I want to die with my baby, give me my baby. I don't have any, you know, how do you say it? I lost my strength and everything. I can't fight anymore. I want to die.

March 16, 1994
Tamarac
JARED: When did you first realize the baby wasn't there anymore?
ALINA: When I didn't hear the cry. I didn't have any more tears, you know? I think I didn't care, I want to die. You know, when comes a minute when you just want to die, you don't want to live anymore, like everything is closing.

Alina reads a sentence aloud from "One Small Candle."

"A little place by yourself, a big tragedy."
You're tired, you're tired, you're sleepy, tired to go on with your life. It's nothing any more.
JARED: Did you see them take the baby away?
ALINA: No, no.
JARED: Were you asleep, or . . .
ALINA: No, I wasn't asleep. She said go on to the bed, I have to walk to the bed. And I was waiting for the baby, and I ask, and

then she gave me this speech. She saved my life, she really saved my life.

evening of January 9, 1993
Tamarac
I myself wonder why I couldn't cry. When I wanted to, I couldn't cry, my tears never came out of my eyes. And all of a sudden I can't stop.

January 9, 1993
Tamarac
ALINA: I remember I want to die with my baby together. You get so, you know, fed up with everything. You didn't want to live. You don't care even, you know. You get some moment, you know, fed up with everything. What I have to fight for? They going to kill me anyway. So better to, you know, to shorten my misery. How you say it, misery?

JARED: Misery.

ALINA: Misery. And I didn't . . . until I got a letter from my husband, you know, when I told you they were looking, the two brothers, my husband and his brother. They didn't know which wife is dead, and I received a letter from him.

That's what keep me a little, you know, give me more strength to go through. Knowing that he's alive, that he's going to make it probably.

April 21, 1993
New Haven
Fortunoff Video Archive at Yale
ALINA: She looked at me, she sat down, she begged me to quiet down and she said, you are so beautiful, you're going to find your husband, you're going to have children, still children.

I still remember the words what she told me. I said, I can't live anymore, I want to die.

Until now I don't know where is my baby.

March 18, 1994
Tamarac
ALINA: Because I didn't see when the baby start to cry . . . stopped to cry. Every day I asked to give me my baby, give me my baby. And then they told me, baby is dead.

JARED: And you always believed that?

ALINA: I didn't think much about it.

JARED: Until when?

ALINA: Like Sophie said to you. One and a half years. But that was before. I didn't speak out, you know. After the war, I talked to my husband. I said, who knows, I'm not sure if my sister is dead, because I wasn't witness to these deaths. So you're never sure, if he's dead or in some other place.

With my mother and father, I have witnesses to it. Because my husband was with my father in the camp and he saw how he's going to the place to die. My mother, it's my cousin, first cousin, came, they let her go to the camp, and she told me about my mother, that my mother went to crematorium.

But the rest, my sister, I don't know, and the baby too, I don't know either.

But then I'm thinking, it was such a hard time in concentration camp. Who would like to raise a baby in such circumstances, right? I am thinking about it. Nobody probably. Like the Russia girl, she didn't want to take it because of beating and no food.

But a lot of times I think about the baby crying.

JARED: Was there ever a moment when you thought about trying to find out?

ALINA: You cannot find out, it's not that easy to find out. You don't have a name. The people around me, they're dead. Some of them dead, some of them went back to Russia. And the Yugoslavia girl, who knows where she is, I don't even know her name. Everything was secret, you don't know anything, the number only.

But I don't remember numbers.

March 16, 1994
Tamarac

ALINA: But now I realize she did a good thing for me.

JARED: This was the Czech woman?

ALINA: Yes. I have the family. I have children. That's the way she brought me. She said, you young. You going to find your husband, and you going to have many children. If I give you the baby, you go with the baby. But I was young, and I didn't understand how I could give the baby without me, you know.

It's like they taking my sense and everything, my body, everything.

* * *

ALINA: And that's what happened. So I was already blaming myself that I brought something to the world. But, you see, you never know if you die or not. You shouldn't decide anything.

It was a beautiful feeling, you know. I'm a mother. I have a baby. And it's like a . . . fruit . . . love . . . you know? I can't explain. But it was a big love, and the fruit from love.

How you say it? Right? I'm saying good? You going to call it different. I don't know.

And it was so beautiful. It was so . . . I have, you know . . . I don't think . . .

So I was thinking about it. The whole nine months what I was pregnant, about the time what I had with my husband. The good time, I mean.

You know who suffer? I'm a mother, and they taking away my love from me. Killing.

March 18, 1994
Tamarac
JARED: So how did you feel on Wednesday, after we talked?
ALINA: I was really sick. Going over things in my mind, and I start to think how the baby looked . . .
JARED: Do you know how the baby looked?
ALINA: Beautiful. A lot of black hair. My husband was blonde, but the baby had my hair. Healthy, compared with the circumstances, with me pregnant in such terrible circumstances, not enough food, and hungry, and everything, yet the baby was healthy.

Never before had Alina mentioned having seen her son.

16

Meeting Ruth

January 8, 1993
Tamarac

JARED: Do you want to talk about that now?

ALINA: No, it's too much. The same time my husband got typhus, I was giving birth to the baby.

JARED: While you were in the hospital did you hear from him often?

ALINA: No, nothing, I didn't hear from him nothing, because they sent him to Buna. They sent him to Buna and I didn't hear from him. But I got a letter from him through a Jewish doctor. He came, and they find out . . . You know, my husband was with his brother together, see? And his wife died. And they found out one of us died. So they thought I died because I was pregnant.

So the doctor came and called my name and he said, who are you?

I said, I am Leo's wife.

And he said, your husband was very sick, he's still sick, he has typhus—he still was in Auschwitz at this time—and he sent a letter to you.

And the letter was like, I didn't even recognize it, like he was a fever, a temperature.

And he asked . . . the doctor, I remember he asked me, what did I have, a girl or a boy?

And I said, son.

He said, girl or boy?

I said, boy.

And he went, and the two brothers were waiting to see who died, his wife or my husband's.

SOPHIA: That is how Jasha found out his wife died?

ALINA: Yes. She died and she was not pregnant, nothing. And she had it good, she had a good job and everything, and she died. And I went through everything and gave birth to a child and I made it.

Buna: A satellite camp of Auschwitz (Auschwitz III), located on the former site of the town of Monowitz and used partly to supply Jewish slave labor to build and run a Buna (synthetic rubber) factory owned by the German chemical company IG Farben.

March 19, 1994
Tamarac

ALINA: *I figured out, I don't remember, but I figured out I gave birth to my child, my baby in December.* After that the *Blockälteste* used to come and pick up people to work, and that is when I went to *Nähstube.*

Nähstube: *sewing workshop.*

March 16, 1994
Tamarac

ALINA: And then I remember the *Blockälteste* came to the barracks to pick up people to work. Okay? And one of them pick me up, and I was so happy to go, because was inside work. Not to go to the 103rd Kommando, to be inside. And the inside was that the clothes came over there and we were fixing them.

April 21, 1993
New Haven
Fortunoff Video Archive at Yale

DANA: Do you remember any friends from this period?

ALINA: Yes, I still have her. I was very close. She lives next to me. I moved to Florida, she moved after. We don't have families, so whoever is alive is like a family. We are very close to each other after, whoever, what we went through. So we are making together sometimes holidays. We are going together, we talk, we cry, we smile together, and it keeps us alive. We help each other a lot.

March 18, 1994
Tamarac

ALINA: You know, she lives here not far away from me.

JARED: Your *Lager*-sister?

ALINA: Yes, *Lager*-sister, Ruth. Her name is Rachelka, her name is Rachelka.

JARED: Rachelka what?

ALINA: I went through with her the whole concentration camp, she was the closer.

JARED: What's her last name?

ALINA: Fontak, this time. But now from the husband she's Kugelman. And she lives not far away from here.

March 19, 1994
Tamarac

JARED: My name is Jared Stark, and I am helping her write a book about her story and Leo's story, and she told me that the two of you went through many of the same experiences, when you met . . .

RUTH FONTAK: We were together from 1944 to 1945 — May the second. We slept together, we ate together, until we came here. Because of her I moved to Tamarac.

JARED: It's nice that you live so close to each other.

March 18, 1994
Tamarac

JARED: You know what would be interesting?

ALINA: Yes?

JARED: I don't know if you'd want to do this with me, or without me . . .

ALINA: Yes?

JARED: . . . but for the two of you, you and your friend, to sit down together with the tape recorder on and to talk.

* * *

JARED: Would she mind?

ALINA: No, she wouldn't mind.

JARED: Would she mind being in the book?

ALINA: I don't think so. I don't think so.

JARED: That would be interesting. Because you have different memories.

ALINA: Yes. I don't have the memory what she has.

JARED: You remember different things.

ALINA: Yes.

JARED: You probably remember some things that she doesn't remember.

ALINA: No, no. I don't remember the dates.

* * *

ALINA: Tell me, I want to ask you something. You want to, you want to have her? You want to talk to her?

JARED: Yes.

ALINA: Yes? When? When?

JARED: Tomorrow?

ALINA: And you will ask the questions, okay? What questions?

JARED: I want to ask her about everything she knows about the same time that she was with you.

ALINA: Yes. What she knows when we were together.

March 19, 1994
Tamarac

JARED: What I am mainly interested in today is from the moment the two of you met and the experiences you shared, and the things . . . like your memory for dates is much sharper than Alina's is.

ALINA: Like evacuation. We start about how we know each other. She mentions *Weberei*, but something happens to me, a feeling that we knowing each other in *Nähstube*.

RUTH: *Nähstube*, no. No, I didn't know Alina then.

Weberei: weavery.

* * *

ALINA: When did you meet me?

RUTH: I met you on the 103rd Kommando.

ALINA: On the 103rd?

RUTH: Yes.

ALINA: For the second time?

RUTH: Yes, for the second time. Then, I met her. We stepped on one ridge, and it so happened that I was standing with a friend of mine, from my town, and with her brother. He came too, and he mentioned a name, Dziedzic.

And I said, what?

Oh, you wouldn't know him because he is from another part of Poland.

ALINA: She had a lot of guts you know.

RUTH: I had an uncle near in Poland, near . . . maybe you know where Vilna is, near the ocean in Poland?

ALINA: Where was the uprising.

RUTH: You know where Poland got the ocean and the port? Near there. He was a very wealthy man, and I was there. Dziedzic is a very uncommon name. This means in Poland a very rich person . . .

ALINA: A farmer.

RUTH: Not farmer, that has horses, he is rich, he is a *dziedzic*. But this was my uncle's name, very unpopular name. And I said, he is from there? I said, yes, my uncle is from there.

dziedzic: *an aristocrat or landowner.*

He said, I am a cousin.

Not knowing me, he gave me cigarettes and sandwiches and I

[81]

shared with her. Then I was only with her, not with the other group as much like with her.

* * *

JARED: Do you know how long you were in the 103rd Kommando?

RUTH: 103rd we were not long. Maybe a month, two months or three months. I'll say three months.

JARED: And this is the point where you met?

RUTH: Yes, I met her there.

ALINA: I remember that I knew her before this.

* * *

RUTH: Then they took us from there to *Weberei*. Then from there . . . we were not long on the 103rd Kommando.

ALINA: We were plenty long. We were long.

RUTH: But not as long.

ALINA: Sure, it seemed shorter because we had more food to eat. Men helped us.

RUTH: Hanka had a Polack who brought sandwiches. You didn't have anybody there.

ALINA: I had the guy who opened the window and pushed the thermos with soup.

April 21, 1993
New Haven
Fortunoff Video Archive at Yale
ALINA: And I was working in *Weberei*. I don't know what is that, the *Weberei*. We were making belts, like you making the hair twists, like challah sometimes . . .

DANA: Oh, braids?

ALINA: Yes, braids, that probably went to the army for something. So it was easier for me than to carry the stones, much easier. But very hard too, very hard.

March 19, 1994
Tamarac
RUTH: When we worked in *Weberei*, we used to go to work in a special barracks for the *Weberei*. Later on, they moved us to one part where all the people in the *Weberei* lived, ate, and worked there, in the same place. We did not go out from there. It was a very bad time

because we couldn't organize anything. Nothing to steal. Organize means stealing, and we couldn't steal anything. Unless someone gave to us.

March 18, 1994
Tamarac

ALINA: I had a guy . . . you know, men were going to work this way and this way, and was a German who was a Kapo, a German Kapo. And he look at me, and next day he gave me a letter from him. You know, a piece of paper in my hand, he pushed to my hand. I came to the barrack that night, and I saw that he's writing, I look like his daughter, all kind of things, you know. And I couldn't stand him because he was a German Kapo. And one time . . .

JARED: What else was he writing to you?

ALINA: That was in *Weberei*, that was in *Weberei*.

JARED: *Weberei*?

ALINA: I was working *Weberei*, I forgot to tell you. We were making belts for the army, something like that.

JARED: When was this?

ALINA: In *Weberei*? That was before, that was in Birkenau. Before evacuation, before evacuation.

JARED: And after the second time you worked under the 103rd Kommando? Or in between the sewing job and the 103rd?

ALINA: I think that's what was. After the sewing, after the sewing, yes.

JARED: And it's called *Weberei*?

ALINA: *Weberei*. That was called *Weberei*.

JARED: What does that mean?

ALINA: Inside. Everybody, every girl was in there and you get, it was making, like, the children having braids . . .

JARED: Yes.

ALINA: That's what we were making. White . . .

JARED: White braids?

ALINA: White like this.

JARED: Out of what?

ALINA: Flat.

JARED: Out of what material?

ALINA: Leather.

JARED: Out of leather?

ALINA: I think this was leather. And so when we came to work . . .

JARED: Was the workplace inside the camp or was it outside the camp?

ALINA: Outside. Everything work was outside.

JARED: The sewing too? Was it outside the camp?

ALINA: What?

JARED: The place where you were fixing the clothes . . .

ALINA: Yes.

JARED: That was outside the camp?

ALINA: No. This was inside. That was inside, yes. See these are little things you know, but . . .

JARED: *Weberei* was outside the camp?

ALINA: . . . *Weberei* was outside.

JARED: Is that a company name? Is that the name of a company?

ALINA: No, this is the name, the work name, *Weberei.* In German, this is *Weberei.* You know, like in English, you going to say . . . when you making something like this from material. How you going to say?

JARED: Piecework?

ALINA: No, not piecework. The name of the work. Like, you knitting, right? And this was *Weberei,* okay?

So, I came and I read the letter, and he said about his daughter and this . . . but next day he came to *Weberei,* to the window—was a window—and he brought a package with food. I think that is in the book. And he brought the package to the window, with food, and my sister, . . . *You know, she lives here not far away from me.*

JARED: *Your* Lager-*sister?*

ALINA: *Yes, my* Lager-*sister, Ruth. Her name is Rachelka, her name is Rachelka.*

JARED: *Rachelka what?*

ALINA: *I went through with her the whole concentration camp, she was the closer.*

JARED: *What's her last name?*

ALINA: *Fontak this time. But now from the husband she's Kugelman. And she lives not far away from here.*

So I couldn't accept that. I could not accept that.

But she said, go, go pick up. You know?

So I said, you go. And she went and pick up the package.

* * *

JARED: Did you call each other sisters in the camp?

ALINA: No, but we were sisters because one can't find her sisters, she wasn't so much close. She was closer to me than to her own sister, because we went through so much together.

March 19, 1994
Tamarac
RUTH: We were six. Alina, Rozka, Itka, Gella, Hanka, and me.
JARED: Who are Gella and Itka?
RUTH: Gella lives in Israel, and these are two sisters and an aunt, and Ala, Hanka, and me. But Hanka wasn't with us at the end anymore.
ALINA: They are from her town.

* * *

JARED: What do you remember about Alina when you first met her?
RUTH: She told me she had a husband here and he used to send her packages but I didn't know her husband. I knew her husband's brother who was looking for his wife.

17

Onions and coffee

March 19, 1994
Tamarac

RUTH: To get back to camp. Later on from the camp, we went . . .
I walked . . . we went on evacuation, January the eighteenth. And we
found a lot of bread we put in knapsacks, the bread, and we were
carrying. And it was very, very cold, and snowing.

And we walked. With Rozka, Rozka was walking by us like that.
Rozka couldn't walk.

ALINA: I was telling, I . . .

RUTH: We carried her under the arms.

ALINA: I told her, I told her the trains were coming. I don't know
how it came to me.

RUTH: So we went to one stop and Hanka said she is not going
anymore. To cover her with the . . .

ALINA: . . . under, under hay.

RUTH: Under hay.

JARED: Where did you find the barn?

RUTH: They put us in a barn. On the way, going there.

JARED: You were spending a night there?

RUTH: And I was so close from my town . . .

ALINA: What was—excuse me, Rachelka, I remember a little
room, and we find onions . . .

RUTH: Where? In the barn?

ALINA: I see a little house, like an apartment.

RUTH: This was where we slept in the attic . . .

JARED: Is this the first night after the evacuation?

RUTH: This is the first night. We slept in the attic, and she says she
is not going. And we couldn't leave her sleeping on the road. This
was so close to my town—with a car, a half an hour. I could have
walked away. But then, where would I go?

ALINA: It's no place. We were afraid of the Polacks.

RUTH: Nobody's there. Nobody's there. And this was in Poland,
in Ober Schlesien. Silesia belongs to Germany . . . it belonged, then.

Ober Schlesien:
Upper Silesia,
region partitioned
between Germany
and Poland after
World War I, now
part of southwestern
Poland.

And I had friends in Katowice, I could have gone to German people. But you have to have guts, you have to have where to go.

As a matter of fact, I have a sister-in-law, from my brother who died, she said to Hanka, Hanka, you cannot walk. Give me . . . She [Hanka] had new shoes that someone gave her, and the shoes were not comfortable for her. She gave it to Lola, Lola gave her her old shoes, and we went.

The next night, we slept in a small house and we found onions, a basket of onions.

ALINA: Yes.

JARED: And you left Hanka in the barn?

RUTH: Under the hay, because she didn't want to walk anymore. She looked like a non-Jewish girl. Blonde, blue-eyed, good-looking.

ALINA: What she said to us? What happened? The Russian came . . .

RUTH: She was there and she was on the farm with the people, and she said she is Polish. And then she went to Katowice, the Russians came in, and to Lodz she went.

JARED: Oh, she told the German people that she was Polish.

RUTH: Yes. Those were Polish people. Because the little town was Polish before. When the Germans came in it was Germany. You know, either way. So, the next night we slept in a little house and we found onions, so everybody ate the onions with the bread. And then the Germans came in . . .

JARED: Were you able to cook them?

ALINA: I remember, I remember . . .

RUTH: No, raw. The German came in, the German what lived in the house, where are my onions? Where's my onions? He was making a big fuss, you know. But, everybody put them away.

JARED: Were there guards traveling with you?

RUTH: Sure.

ALINA: They were shooting whoever was in . . .

RUTH: If you did not walk, if you sat down, they shoot you. So you were not allowed to sit.

JARED: How many women were there?

RUTH: Oh, there was thousands, thousands.

ALINA: The highway was covered with us.

RUTH: With us, with people. Then we . . .

JARED: Did many die?

RUTH: Yes, yes, on the sides, and . . .

ALINA: . . . all over.

RUTH: And they had such a stick with a special . . .

ALINA: To shoot from . . .

RUTH: To shoot from . . . I don't know, what the hell you call it? My husband would know the name of the stick, and on the top was like a big balloon on it.

JARED: For what?

ALINA: A weapon, I don't know, it was kind of like, you throw . . .

JARED: Like a spear?

ALINA: Not spear, but to blow up.

RUTH: Do you want a coffee?

JARED: Yes, I'll have a little coffee.

RUTH: And you, Ala?

ALINA: Okay.

JARED: Like a grenade?

ALINA: Yes, looks like a grenade.

RUTH: No, this was not a grenade.

ALINA: I don't know, I don't remember no more. I remember when we were in the little house, the apartment, I felt so . . . everything was wet and I took off my stockings. I was wearing, like, socks, and I hang it up. And as soon as I hang it up they call to start walking.

RUTH: What kind of coffee do you want?

ALINA: Regular.

RUTH: Or decaffeinated?

ALINA: And he'll have regular. Whatever you have. So that's what I remember. And was, I was so miserable that we have to start again to walk. And my feet was so cold.

JARED: So you didn't get to put your stockings back on?

ALINA: No, I didn't, I didn't have a chance.

JARED: Did you take them with you?

ALINA: No, what the use to take them? And we walked and we walked. And I said that the trains are coming. Rose, Rozka Londner, got the same sickness what Hanka got, okay? And she had, she had terrible pains in her groin and she couldn't walk. We took her under arm, we took everything . . . So that's what I remember.

What happened then, I start to say, I think I hear the trains coming.

JARED: Did you hear them or did you just say that?

Just as Ruth returns with the coffee, her husband and sister-in-law return home. The tape is interrupted briefly while I meet Ruth's family.

ALINA: No. I made up stories so that she should have more strength to go through it.

* * *

[88]

JARED: We left off on the second night after the evacuation.

RUTH: Well, we slept in this room and the German came in for the onions. Where are mine onions? Like the world falls apart. And we were laughing. We were in such a trouble, we couldn't sleep, we were tired.

So then we walked again. We walked, we came in, in a big warehouse, where they kept the wheat . . .

JARED: Do you have all the same memories?

RUTH: . . . they kept the wheat.

ALINA: I have different, I have different memories.

RUTH: You don't have those memories?

ALINA: Like what?

RUTH: We went out from the house, we came—

ALINA: I told you about the onions—

JARED: And the German coming in?

ALINA: Right, right.

RUTH: And we have to go to the big warehouse. We slept there, and from there we went to the wagons that were standing waiting for us.

ALINA: I remember I was in the room.

RUTH: Which room?

ALINA: They came. Some room, I remember.

RUTH: Where?

ALINA: In house.

RUTH: We were together in a little room.

ALINA: Yes. Do you remember when I have my socks wet? And I hang up?

RUTH: Yes, but did it get dry?

ALINA: No, they came, that what I'm saying. How soon I took off my socks . . .

RUTH: He came and . . .

ALINA: . . . he came and I had to leave my socks, and without socks . . .

JARED: So you didn't even spend the night there?

RUTH: I don't think so. We went out. They threw us out.

ALINA: Yes, we went out. You know what they do to us? The Russians started to come. How closer they were, they [the Germans] were pushing us.

JARED: Did you know they were coming?

ALINA: Yes.

RUTH: Hey, Rozka . . . hey, Ala. The German, the owner from the house, didn't want us, he threw us out.

ALINA: He couldn't do nothing.

JARED: Then where did you go?

RUTH: He was the owner!

ALINA: No, he couldn't . . .

JARED: So where did you go when he threw you out?

RUTH: So we went on the road, and we went the next night, we slept in a big, big storage, for wheat or something there. And from there we went to the . . .

ALINA: Was it a barn?

RUTH: A barn. A big, a storage, big. Tremendous big.

ALINA: Yes, I remember that.

RUTH: . . . and we slept on the top. And next, a day later, the wagons were standing, like for cattle.

JARED: Right there next to the barn?

ALINA: No, we walked, because we were walking with Rozka.

RUTH: No, this was before. We walked all the way with Rozka, who couldn't walk.

ALINA: Right.

JARED: Do you know what town this was near?

RUTH: I will tell you, this was in Silesia, Poland, but belonged to Germany, Silesia.

ALINA: They were pushing us back . . .

RUTH: . . . and we went there. From there we went in the open cattle wagons. I found a corner, sat in corner near the wall, because it was comfortable. We sat on the meal sacks, on the bread.

JARED: Where did you get all the bread?

RUTH: From Auschwitz. On the road, the Polish people, the German people, gave us some water, on the road. But the German didn't let. Then we met a girl walking with a can of milk. A little can, and we grabbed it from her. And I got the can, and I got it with me. So, to have water from ice, we put it in the can. We ate the bread, it was just crumbs, because if you sit on bread it gets crumbs. We couldn't eat it, we were so thirsty.

We couldn't go to a toilet. There was no toilet. And two soldiers were in every wagon with us.

JARED: In the wagons?

RUTH: Yes. We came to . . .

JARED: How many people were in a wagon?

RUTH: I don't know. About forty, fifty, sixty. It was so crowded. We were sitting in the middle, we couldn't sleep because one was laying on the other. But when we had the corner near the wall at least we had support.

ALINA: This is when we went to . . .

RUTH: Ravensbrück.

ALINA: Ravensbrück? I remember closed trains.

RUTH: If you remember closed trains . . . Oh, that is what she remembers—from Ravensbrück to Neustadt-Glewe, we had closed passenger trains. But you are mixing up.

ALINA: Right.

JARED: But this was open cattle cars?

ALINA: Right. Open cattle trains to Ravensbrück.

JARED: No roof?

RUTH: No roof, and it happened that it did not snow. But after some German soldiers give us some snow, there was water. We came, I remember, to Frankfurt . . .

JARED: Did they give you snow?

RUTH: Yes. He was not . . . he was the *Wehrmacht*. They were . . . by themselves they were tired, too. So when we stopped, he went down, and pushing some snow.

ALINA: *Wehrmacht* wasn't a member . . .

JARED: Did you stop to pick up more people?

RUTH: No, we were full already.

ALINA: . . . *Wehrmacht* was people . . .

RUTH: He knows what the *Wehrmacht* is.

ALINA: . . . what wasn't member of Nazi . . .

RUTH: This was not a party member.

We came to Frankfurt-an-Oder.

JARED: How long did that take?

RUTH: About two days, one day, next day. Because this is not far, this is in Ober Schlesien too. And I see German women, like nurses, giving coffee. So I gave her my hand to give us coffee. And she gave us coffee, and this a Gestapo man saw. And he came in, and he said, who got the coffee? Who got the coffee? So the German soldier took away my can and took the can and threw it away, with the coffee.

And while we were in—remember this? You don't remember this?

ALiNA: I don't remember this, no.

RUTH: And while we were there some trains were coming from Germany with German people, evacuate the part they were bombarded. They were in different directions, but we asked them for a cigarette. Nobody could give us a cigarette.

Then after two nights, two days traveling in the train we came to Ravensbrück. Big concentration camp. Tremendous big.

And I think we got stronger

18

January 13, 1985
The Hartford Courant
When her child was born the women would not let Alina near it because she had again fallen ill with the fever. For four days she listened to her baby crying and finally it died. Shortly thereafter, Alina was transferred to Ravensbrück, and then to Neustadt-Glewe.

March 18, 1994
Tamarac
JARED: So what happened when you first arrived in Ravensbrück?
ALINA: Oh, I start to tell you. So they put us there, and they didn't send us to work, and they didn't give us to eat. And the kitchen was very close, you know, like the building over there. And it was so, they taking out the big . . . how do you call where soup is inside?
JARED: The kettle?
ALINA: Kettle?
JARED: Like a soup kettle?
ALINA: Yes, from metal. This is from metal. And they taking out the soup, and other people are coming, and taking, and spreading around to the blocks, to the barracks, and we didn't get anything.

So the next day, you know what we did? When they took out the soup, we took the soup, we brought ourselves to our block. I don't know. Nobody have spoons, nobody have anything. But I don't know, everybody find something to grab something and eat. And after that, they sent us to Neustadt-Glewe. What we realize, I think they got scared of uprising or something.
JARED: How long were you in Ravensbrück?
ALINA: Not too long, because we didn't work there.
JARED: More like . . . three days, a month?
ALINA: I have to find out. Let me call my friend to find out. She remember.

* * *

JARED: When you arrived at Ravensbrück, were there women there already?

ALINA: Yes. The first time I saw black people, from French colony. First time in my life I was learning about them. I saw picture in the book, I never saw them. First time I saw black people in Ravensbrück.

JARED: What did you think?

ALINA: I don't know. I was . . . you know, the hard time make you stronger, I think so. You got used not to eat, you got used to, you know, to get beaten up, you just watching not to get it, but if you . . .

And we were, you know, to pass the time we always talk about our family, of what my mother used to cook . . . And everybody was talking, and we were eating that in our minds. And I think we got stronger. More experience we had.

March 19, 1994
Tamarac

JARED: Did you know in the camps about Alina's baby?

RUTH: No. She told me the story.

JARED: When did she tell you?

RUTH: When I met her, at the very beginning.

JARED: Had you heard any other stories like that?

RUTH: From other people? No. This is one of a kind.

JARED: What did you think about it when you heard it?

RUTH: Tragedy. I know they took all the pregnant woman to the crematorium. They ask you when you came in, when you arrived to Birkenau, who is pregnant? They are going to have special care. So they signed up.

ALINA: They used to tell them . . .

JARED: Do you remember her telling you about this for the first time?

RUTH: I remember when she told me this what happened. She was in a different block and there was a Polish girl, the *Blockälteste*. She was the supervisor from the block, she saved her.

* * *

RUTH: So we went out from Ravensbrück. They gave us salami. And we were in passenger wagons and a German, a woman, she was watching us on the train. We were so thirsty that we asked her to go down in the station and get us water, and she did. She was very nice. You see, in this camp, the German people, how do you call this? This is what took care of us, she took care of us . . .

ALINA: . . . the *Aufseherin.*

RUTH: They were not such rules, not such a mean, like from Auschwitz-Birkenau. This was special, they taught them to go with the dogs, to be mean, nasty, to kill us, they were killers. But this one, what's her name?

ALINA: We didn't have really too long contact with them.

RUTH: That's right . . . this was six weeks after. So after, we were February, March they sent us to Neustadt-Glewe. We came to this camp, Neustadt-Glewe . . .

JARED: How long did it take to get there?

RUTH: Hours. Not far away. Ravensbrück is not far from Berlin.

ALINA: It was few hours.

RUTH: Hours. We came to this camp, this crazy camp.

* * *

RUTH: There were thousands of people there. And in this camp there used to be Polish women, from Warsaw uprising. The Polish people made an uprising in 1944, in Warsaw.

ALINA: Where my sister died.

RUTH: And they took the Polish women and sent them to this camp, to Neustadt-Glewe. But when we came, they took them out to another camp, and they put us in. They couldn't supply the people with food. And the commander from this camp walked around with a gun, because the people were wild.

ALINA: We were hungry, everybody hungry, and nothing to eat.

19 Liberation

March 19, 1994
Tamarac

Chef: *camp commander.*

RUTH: The *Chef* from the camp, he happened to be a nice guy. The food was very limited already.

We were standing around and he said like this—he showed with the hand—Germany used to be a big, big country. Now it is very little, very little food. That's not going to take long, be prepared, it's going to end very soon, he said it to us.

And people from Ravensbrück, all the soldiers, they start to run, because the Americans, the Russians . . .

JARED: From Ravensbrück?

RUTH: Yes, from Ravensbrück they came to our camp. They brought clothes for us to wash them. We felt it was the end of the war.

ALINA: Because we saw the next day everybody disappeared, there was nobody, only the leaflets . . .

April 21, 1993
New Haven
Fortunoff Video Archive at Yale

ALINA: So they put us in trains, and that was my last concentration camp. It was Neustadt-Glewe, where I was liberated from both, Russians and Americans over there. Then the Americans moved away, and they have some different side, but the Russian soldiers stayed. And we decide to go to Poland to look for family, whoever is alive.

DANA: Do you remember the liberation day as such? Can you tell us what happened that day?

ALINA: I am going to tell you that I thought I'm getting crazy, you know. Because before we find out, I don't know that was Russian or American, throwing leaflets from the plane. And we wasn't allowed even to pick them up, because the Germans were still in the camp.

And maybe two minutes later, five minutes later, we didn't see Germans around.

And we run out and we say, probably they lost the war and they running away.

You know, we were hungry, so we have a friend, my friend, close friend, we called *Lager*-sister. She was working in the laundry, and from the laundry was an opening like a window. And she saw over there like a *Magazin* with Red Cross packages. They were keeping there, but they didn't give us anything.

Magazin: storehouse.

We managed to go to break through the window and everybody started to open the packages from Red Cross, and taking out. And we organized. You take flour, I will take cigarettes, I take sugar, so everyone has something.

I went on top of the garbage dump, and I looked out, and I thought I'm getting crazy. I couldn't talk, I couldn't smile, I couldn't do nothing.

March 19, 1994
Tamarac

ALINA: Everybody had to pick up something else from the packages. You pick up cigarettes, I pick up sugar . . .

RUTH: We picked up the whole packages . . .

ALINA: Not the whole packages . . . because there was a mess of people in the front gate, okay? So we were going with the front gate and she knew how to go to the other side, to the . . .

RUTH: No, I went to the laundry room . . .

ALINA: That is what I am saying. You don't hear me. That is what I said. Everybody started to push in the front.

RUTH: This was May second, the day of liberation. As a matter of fact, May the first, they start to run out, the Germans. They closed the camp. I said, hey you, the laundry, why don't you come and pick it up? And they were running, and we were all left alone. And so we went in the kitchen and started to grab whatever we could.

ALINA: No, we were talking to each other, you take this, because there was a mess of people. They broke the front door and everybody made that we should not have everything the same. Each one picked up something different.

RUTH: So you remember better.

ALINA: You don't remember that?

RUTH: This is not important, believe me.

* * *

RUTH: So I almost fainted from all the pushing, pulling, and I almost fainted, and I never fainted in the life. So we moved out from our quarters and we moved into the German quarters. We were in three beds, we were six girls, we slept two girls in each bed. And we went on the town.

* * *

ALINA: Because they came, you know, from one side from Russia, and from the other side, the Americans.

RUTH: The Americans liberated us. We didn't see any soldiers. We went to town, full of German soldiers sitting with the guns, with everything, but we were not afraid of them anymore because they were powerless.

JARED: You still hadn't seen American soldiers, though?

RUTH: No, I came to town and saw the American soldiers. We went over and we showed them . . .

ALINA: They were drinking on the tanks together.

RUTH: No, don't mix up two stories. This was the [Russians] came in with tanks. American soldiers came in without anything. Light shoes, nice light faces. It was May, it was warm.

We told them we were from the concentration camps and they didn't know what we were talking about. We found a Jewish guy with a star, and he couldn't speak Jewish, we couldn't speak English. Even a guy wanted to come over and give me a kiss. I said, hey, you, "gentleman"! This I knew, my father was in America. I knew "baby," "money," these things. I said, "gentleman."

We went into the hotel where they were there, and they pulled out drawers for clothes. We pulled it out, they pushed it in.

So we are going for bread, where are we going? To the grocery, or the bakery. The baker is closed—full of people—the bakery was closed, the window was open, we went to the window and took out the bread. The German people looked like we crazy. They didn't understand this.

Schmaltz herring: preserved high-fat herring.

We went into the grocery and we took some schmaltz herring, eggs, and they didn't say one word, the Germans.

We went to the milk man, where he delivered milk to the camps, and I said, give us the milk and the cans.

And he said, but you have to bring them back, and we promised we're going to bring them back

And Rozka saw a chicken, she grabbed the chicken and killed the chicken. I couldn't do this, she took off the head.

We brought all these things back and she cooked the first dinner.   *Ruth points to Alina.*

JARED: Do you remember cooking it?

ALINA: Borscht . . .

RUTH: Borscht with potatoes . . .

ALINA: . . . with potatoes and chicken. And I remember I started to sew dresses from the tablecloths.

April 21, 1993
New Haven
Fortunoff Video Archive at Yale

ALINA: And we moved to the barracks what the SS was sleeping there. We found a little oven, a standing oven with a pipe going out from it, and I remember the first dinner I made. We found potatoes there, I made, and borscht.

We start to throw everything what we were wearing. We were taking the tablecloths and I was making dresses for everybody. We were free, and I was planning to go to Warsaw, and they were planning to go to Katowice.

March 19, 1994
Tamarac

RUTH: Yes, they came and they liberated us. They came from the Elbe, and they came to Berlin, and they met, this was the meeting point. We were in the middle.

And the minute the Russians came, they said to us in Russian—we understood because it is similar to Polish—girls, you need something, you go to the Germans and you take anything you want. This was the best there was.

ALINA: Yes, yes.

RUTH: So we went. We went up the tanks and they kissed, the Americans with the Russians. They hugged and kissed, but they couldn't talk to each other. And the Americans were on the tanks, we were on the tanks, and they were on the tanks, and they took out cans. It was sardines they ate. They started to drink.

And we went to the houses, what did we take? We were stupid. We could have taken anything, but we took food. Marmalade, jelly.

ALINA: Salami.

RUTH: Not salami. Was there salami?

JARED: Why do you say you were stupid?

RUTH: Because we could have taken expensive pictures, expensive stuff. We didn't take, because we were hungry. So we took it all and put it in a little wagon. And the Russians helped us pull the wagons, with the food, with the marmalade, home.

JARED: Where did you pull the wagon to?

RUTH: A little wagon like for children . . .

JARED: Where did you go?

RUTH: To our camp, where we lived. The Russians said, you know what, we are going to be in the forest here, and the Americans moved out and the Russians stayed. They moved over the Elbe.

* * *

JARED: Did they [the Russians] know what the concentration camps were?

RUTH: They knew. They killing on the way. They raped and they killed and they murdered. The Germans were so afraid of the Russians you can't even imagine. They didn't leave a house whole. They did everything. They went through hell there too, the Germans.

ALINA: They had war before that with Germany, you know.

RUTH: There was a long way to go when they came. We figured they were nice guys, but you have some mixture of people in Russia from all different directions. Like, Cossacks, and the ones with the Mongolian eyes, animals . . . And they said they are having a party in the forest. All girls, come!

So we were maybe twenty girls, we went there. They were singing and laughing and they put salamis, and fried them with eggs, and they gave us vodka to drink. We were happy, they took us home nicely, everyone was drunk.

Later on they came and they wanted to rape the girls. We had a night. I was yelling—one was with a gun—I was yelling—we didn't have lights, only candles—I blew out the candles, I was jumping from the bed and running and screaming, yelling until he ran out. When I came out, she was with another girl out there and she was altogether drunk.

ALINA: I was? Who?

RUTH: Rozka was drunk outside.

ALINA: Oh yes, but I was with Rozka's sister.

JARED: Did you go to the party too, Alina?

RUTH: No, she didn't go to the party.

March 15, 1994
Tamarac
Because I act different than everybody else when I find out I am free.

And we miss each other

20

April 21, 1993
New Haven
Fortunoff Video Archive at Yale
ALINA: I was lucky. I find my husband after the war. I didn't know for three months if he is alive.

March 18, 1994
Tamarac
JARED: When did you first see him again?

ALINA: My husband?

JARED: Yes. Where were you?

ALINA: I found out that he is alive, you know how. And how soon I find out he's alive, the guy begs me, go, because he is sick. He told me he's going to look for me when he's going to be healthy in Germany, for me, and then he should look in Poland for me.

JARED: Leo?

ALINA: Yes, Leo.

JARED: How did you feel when you first heard that he was alive?

ALINA: I don't know. I sometimes think is something wrong with me. It's something I can't be happy. If I'm happy, I'm not showing. I am happy, but I cannot show. But when he told me, I was so happy I was sitting crying, I start to cry, you know? Because I find my husband is alive. And I was very happy, and I wait for the moment.

But what was, I sent him a picture and letter to tell him and to show him that I'm alive, okay, and I'm coming . . . that I'm alive. I didn't write that I'm coming.

When he received the letter, he didn't wait. He went to Poland for me. And I went to him. And we miss each other.

April 21, 1993
New Haven
Fortunoff Video Archive at Yale
ALINA: I was in Katowice with my friends. My friends find two brothers, and they have apartment over there, and we have where to sleep.

And one evening somebody came from Bergen-Belsen, and my friend introduced me as her sister, Alina Bakalczuk from Warsaw.

He look at me and he said, do you have a husband, Leo Bakalczuk? I said, sure, this is my husband.

And he said, you know, this is a letter from your husband to you. He is very sick.

He was very sick in Bergen-Belsen when the war finished.

March 18, 1994
Tamarac

JARED: Maybe you can tell me about when you first found Leo again.

ALINA: When, now?

JARED: No, then.

ALINA: She find first, then me.

JARED: She found him first?

ALINA: He went to look for me.

JARED: Yes.

ALINA: She going to tell you that. You going to laugh. You going to get a comedy, yes.

March 19, 1994
Tamarac

RUTH: It was funny. I'll tell you this, this was the end of the war. I see a man comes in and I say, are you Bacall — Bakalczuk?

ALINA: Yes, after the war.

RUTH: After the war, in Katowice, we were sitting there having coffee and ice cream, and he didn't have money and I paid for him.

ALINA: He got Russian money.

RUTH: He had ten rubles, Russian silver . . . gold . . . or something. He had to change it. So I paid for him. He still owes me

Ruth chuckles. this . . .

March 18, 1994
Tamarac

ALINA: Rachelka, my friend, recognized him. She said, that must be Ala's husband.

JARED: Just from your verbal description?

ALINA: Yes, right.

JARED: How did you describe him?

ALINA: Blonde with blue eyes. And he's friendly guy, everybody likes him, and he has lots of people. You know, very, very nice person. Easy going.

JARED: Did you describe him in more detail physically?

ALINA: Yes.

JARED: What else did you say about him? How did you describe him to your friends?

ALINA: He's good looking, handsome, very. And . . . you saw the picture.

JARED: I know, but how did you describe him?

ALINA: How tall I said he is, but I don't remember how tall he was. But he was average. And he was nice build, but not fat. Nice build. And the complexion, he always had the beautiful complexion, like rosy complexion. White, you know, white skin, good complexion. And the nose was a little up, I said. Blue eyes, nice eyelashes, and curly hair. Blonde, curly hair. Not curly, but wavy. So when he walk in, they knew who this is.

April 21, 1993
New Haven
Fortunoff Video Archive at Yale

ALINA: And I find where he is.

So when this guy what we save him, what the Russian people want to kill him—his name was Salek—he came to say goodbye and he's telling me that he is going to Bergen-Belsen.

And I said, Salek, you know, I find out that my husband is alive, you will take my picture—because it was so hard to believe that somebody is alive—my picture I give you and a few words to my husband.

He said, are you kidding? You saved my life, I will do it. And he went there, and he gave him the letter and the picture.

Meanwhile, my husband's . . . my brother-in-law came from Theresienstadt, and he was very sick after typhus. And he came and he said, I hear that Leo is not alive, that my husband is not alive.

I said, no, he is alive.

He couldn't believe it. I have to take him to this guy who brought me the good news.

And I said, you know, I'm going tomorrow to my husband.

He said, I'm sick. I can't go.

I said, all right. So you're going to stay here, and I'm going to go. But finally he decided he would go with me.

Warsaw Ghetto Resistance Organization

Commemoration Journal: Forty-second Anniversary of the Warsaw Ghetto Uprising, 1943–1985

My name is Jack Bacall of New York. I was born in Warsaw as Jasha Bakalczuk. I survived the Warsaw ghetto and many camps, including Auschwitz, Majdanek, Buchenwald, Sachsenhausen, and Grevinkel.

I was liberated at the war's end in Litmeric, Czechoslovakia. However, my family was not that fortunate. My father died of a heart attack during the occupation when the Nazis came to the house to take the children to forced labor. My mother and older sister were the first to be deported. Of our family of eight—my parents, four brothers, and two sisters—only myself and my brother, Leo, have survived.

March 18, 1994
Tamarac
JARED: How did you get there?
ALINA: Walking . . . first of all we took the train.
JARED: You were with his brother?
ALINA: Open train.
JARED: You were with his brother?

ALINA: Right, open. Everything open, and we ate . . . I jump from a train. He was at the time very weak and I was jumping from freight.

JARED: Why did you have to jump from the train?

ALINA: To pick up some fruit. The train was moving like this . . . this wasn't a train, this was a freight train.

JARED: Were many people on the train?

ALINA: Only we two. They were carrying coals, and we were sitting on the coals, and whenever I saw a tree with fruit I jumped, because it was going slow, and get some pears or apples, and we were eating. Then we would get back.

JARED: Then you would jump back on the train?

ALINA: Yes.

JARED: While it was moving?

ALINA: Yes. If you saw me like this . . . I can't believe it. I was doing that.

April 21, 1993
New Haven
Fortunoff Video Archive at Yale

ALINA: You know how we go? With the trains, the trains what they carry coals. And we were jumping on the coals and this way the train was going. In Germany you have the fruit trees on the highway, and I jumped, because he was sick, took some fruit, went back to the wagon, until we went to Prague, in Czechoslovakia. Over there is already, this is Russian side, and then we have to try to get to English side because Bergen-Belsen was in English hands. So, I am coming there and we had to wait to find out how to go through the Russian and to him, finally we made it, we made it.

And I'm coming to my husband, but I hear my husband got the letter and picture and he left for Katowice, for Poland. And we missed each other.

March 18, 1994
Tamarac

ALINA: He sent a telegraph from Prague that he is coming back. And I wait and wait. And he came . . .

JARED: To Bergen-Belsen?

ALINA: Yes. And I said, I'm probably going to jump on him from the window when he is coming. And I sit there and wait and wait until he came to me.

April 21, 1993
New Haven
Fortunoff Video Archive at Yale

ALINA: So I have to wait another month maybe, or two, until he came. And that was something. I was like stone. Something stayed in me, you know. I'm very happy but I can't show a lot. I cannot cry if it's tragedy. Only after a while, day or two. So many times my kids say, mommy are you not happy? I say, I am happy, I am very happy, but I just can't show the feeling. Can't show.

March 18, 1994
Tamarac

JARED: So immediately you started to tell each other your stories, what had happened to you?

ALINA: Yes, everything, what had happened to the family. We start to talk, everything. We were talking about how I came, you know, from Poland to here.

* * *

JARED: So how long did the two of you spend in Bergen-Belsen?

ALINA: Not too long because we didn't have a place. I don't know how, he went to somebody, like the English people, soldier, and he got a bicycle, before I came. He said he found my wife and I would like to have bicycle. You know, he wasn't shy. He went to the soldiers and said, I found my wife, she is alive, and I would like to have a bicycle for me and for her. So they gave it to him. So I have a bicycle. I never rode a bicycle in my life. So one day . . . do you have this story?

JARED: I think you told it to me, but go ahead, continue . . .

ALINA: Yes? I was riding, I knew everything, but how to stop I didn't know. When he told me, stop, I said, I don't know how to stop. And he was teaching me and I want to do something. Maybe I stopped too fast, and I find myself . . . But nothing happened to me. That's the way I learned how to stop.

* * *

JARED: What did Leo tell you the first time he saw you?

ALINA: He was very happy. He loved me very much. And he wants to find out, we start to talk about the baby. And he told me what I don't know, he start to tell me about . . .

The tape comes to an end.

From Marburg to America

April 21, 1993
New Haven
Fortunoff Video Archive at Yale

DANA: How did you find your sister?

ALINA: My sister? A friend of my husband came and told him that he read a Jewish paper and somebody is looking for me, and I find out it was my sister.

SUSAN: Where were you then?

ALINA: In Germany. She was in Poland. I didn't know that she was in Poland. I went to Warsaw, and she didn't register herself that she is looking for anybody, because she was a hundred percent sure nobody was alive. So, all of a sudden a rabbi from Warsaw passed the street. I didn't know him, but he said, I saw your sister with her husband, and they went to Germany. Maybe my husband saw him on the street. And that is what she decided to go to Germany to look for me.

I was with George nine months pregnant, and when I find out that my sister is alive I start to go to her. I hear she's in, this time, in Stuttgart I think, in Germany, and my husband took me and we went over there, and she wasn't there anymore.

Finally, she managed to find out where I am and she came to me, and she stayed in Marburg with us. I find a nice husband for her, a friend of ours, and introduced to her. And they start to go together, got married. She have two beautiful children. So the family is a little bigger now.

March 18, 1994
Tamarac

JARED: After that, you had to decide . . . you tried to go to Israel? Or you tried to go to the United States?

ALINA: We tried to come to Israel but they didn't let us go. I was pregnant with Georgie and we would have to come not legal. Remember, the English stopped the boat? Didn't let . . . brought them to Cyprus.

Between August 13, 1946, and February 10, 1949, the British government stopped thirty-nine boats carrying Jewish refugees, many of them survivors of the Holocaust, from reaching Palestine. Twelve detention camps were established on the island of Cyprus, where refugees spent from a few months to two years in harsh and crowded conditions. Over fifty-two thousand Jews passed through the Cyprus detention camps.

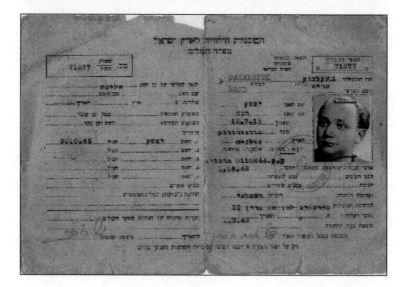

Alina's and Leo's registration certificates from the Jewish Agency for Palestine.

When he saw me, he said, no, you cannot go.

So I said, I can't stay here.

You know, my husband tried to open a store there, a textile store. You know that, right?

JARED: Yes, you told me that.

ALINA: Yes. I couldn't stand it. I saw blood in every stone there in Germany. I didn't want to stay there.

April 21, 1993
New Haven
Fortunoff Video Archive at Yale

ALINA: This was a nice little town there. And we got an apartment, and he tried to open a store. And he had a hard time because he was a Polish Jew. The German Jew got the store and the stamps and they could settle, and my husband couldn't get it because he was a Polish Jew.

Ausländer-Ausweis
Certificate for Foreigners
Nationality: polish (Jude)

April 21, 1993
New Haven
Fortunoff Video Archive at Yale

So he came one day and he said, I am not going to move from here. I was discriminated because I am a Jew, now you discriminate me because I'm a Polish Jew. And I'm going to get this store. I'm not going to move from here.

They gave him the store, he opened it, in textiles, because he was in textiles.

Ausländer-Ausweis
Certificate for Foreigners
It is requested to treat bearer of this certificate favourably.

Storefront of A.G.B. (Alinka und Gebrüder Bakalczuk), the textile shop opened by Leo and his brother, Jasha, in Marburg.

Translated from German by George Bacall.

To all clothing manufacturers and textile wholesalers
Minister for Political Freedom
Hessian State Ministry
May 13, 1947
Weisbaden, Germany

The firm A.G.B, owned by the brothers Bakalczuk, Marburg/Lahn, has a license to operate a fabric store, haberdashery, clothing store, and dressmaker. The owners of this firm belong to the group of the racially persecuted. It is my commission to oversee the Jewish communities as well as the bureau for the politically, racially, and religiously persecuted.

In order to give the owners of this firm the opportunity to establish itself, I ask you to include them among your preferred customers and also to give them preferential supply of goods.

March 18, 1994
Tamarac

ALINA: And we got from Nazis, they took from Nazis, was a mother with two sons, and they put her in one room and they give us two rooms, was three rooms, I don't know. She had one or two. Anyway, like we shared the apartment together with her. That was our first place to live.

JARED: Was she nice to you?

ALINA: Yes. We were nice to her, too. Her husband was a big Nazi. He wasn't alive. Maybe in some other place, running. But nice, we had a big room. I had my baby Georgie there in this apartment.

Marburg,
Germany, 1947.

April 21, 1993
New Haven
Fortunoff Video Archive at Yale

ALINA: Oh, this is my son born in Germany, my first son. Not first, second. The first . . .

This is picture of my child in Germany, George.

* * *

ALINA: And I was so afraid to have a child. He wants family, and I said, for what? Again going to happen, again they're going to kill our

children. I was so afraid always. I got my son, I was pregnant with a second child and I didn't want it. I was afraid, again.

And I said to my husband, I don't want to have a child anymore. I hate to be in Germany, I hate all the Germans, I can't stand the stones, it's covered with blood, everything is in blood.

If he was thinking to have a baby, I was angry at him. And I said, fine, I'm going to go and look how to get rid of the baby, and I went, and I got rid.

March 18, 1994
Tamarac
ALINA: I was feeding my baby, Georgie, and I didn't feel good, so I went to check myself and they told me I was pregnant. Very easy for me to get pregnant. And I said to my husband, I'm pregnant. And he said, beautiful, beautiful. I said, I don't want to have this child. He begged me and I said, no! And it was very hard this time to get diapers and everything.

* * *

JARED: Was abortion legal?
ALINA: I don't know even, maybe not? Maybe yes, who knows.
JARED: But you were awake through the whole . . .
ALINA: I was waiting for somebody who makes abortion, and my husband got scared I would go to wrong place. So he got people, connections to find out, to find a professor who is making that in Eschenberg in the hospital.

That was wintertime, too. We were coming back with the car, we almost got accident because it was slippery. In Germany the streets are round, turn around, and we almost went down a cliff, but in the last minute the car stopped.

And he said to me . . . and I was sick, because after that I went to the car, we were going back to Marburg-an-der-Lahn from Eschenberg.

JARED: From Eschenberg?

ALINA: From Eschenberg.

So what happened, he said, see, God punished us. Because we did that to the child, God punished us.

We were lucky, they start to spread the salt because it was very icy, and sand. So he took from me the blanket what I had around me and put under the tire. This I will never forget, I was scared to death. And they put sand and he started . . . he was afraid to stop because it was on the edge. When I'm thinking about it I am getting scared.

JARED: Did you stay in the car?

ALINA: Yes, in the car because he didn't let me come out because it was freezing, and after the operation, everything, I was sick.

JARED: Did you stay in the hospital overnight?

ALINA: No, just to make the abortion and then I went back to the car. And to have the pains, they didn't give me to sleep anything, nothing. So it was a little hard for me.

January 8, 1993
Tamarac

JARED: Where was George born?

ALINA: George was born in Germany. When I came with him here he was two years old, he was almost three years. 1946 I think he was born, because we came here in 1949. He was almost three years old. I remember I have to wait in Germany because they had to take the tonsils out. He was born in '46.

March 18, 1994
Tamarac

JARED: What did you know about the United States before you came here?

ALINA: That I have to work hard. I didn't have the language. And I said, I'm ready for it. I couldn't stand it in Germany.

JARED: Did you think of going back to Poland?

ALINA: No, I hate Poland too.

April 21, 1993
New Haven
Fortunoff Video Archive at Yale

ALINA: I was a different person when I came to the United States. I worked so hard. I went to school. I cleaned the house. I cook after work. I came home and I cook for the next day, and nothing was hard for me. Everything was fine, because compared to what we went through . . .

And I remember what I promised myself, and whatever I had was good, and I am happy. But, just I can't show too much.

Memorials

22

March 15, 1994
Tamarac

ALINA: It was raining. We had umbrellas with us. I remember I find for you umbrella, too. And it was like my heart, you know? The feeling was like the weather. But I was very happy to be there.

Usually I don't like to go, you know? Since I . . . but I was very happy I was there, because . . . because I saw people, you know, stick out for, you know, for the people what are dead. Like between them is my mother, my family, my child. Everybody's dead. And I felt this is my cemetery, this is going to be my cemetery.

JARED: And you felt happy to see your cemetery?

ALINA: That's my family, who have place now, because, you know, like somebody die from your family, you know? They lay in care, they have cemetery, they have graves, right? On holidays, if you want to go and . . . like, just to talk, just to talk to myself . . . it's like a private thing. I never have my mother's grave, nobody's. Now I have. If I want to talk to them, I go, I go there.

April 21, 1993
New Haven
Fortunoff Video Archive at Yale

ALINA: I came, finally, to the United States, my son was two and a half years, and then took me another six years to have another child.

Now, again, I'm worried, what's going on in this world. My gosh, look at it. In Yugoslavia, nobody say a word about anything, quiet, like we were killed and nobody knew about it. They knew, but they didn't speak out. They didn't want to do anything about us.

The only thing, I'm happy now when I'm thinking, I'm going to Washington, to the museum tomorrow. And the children are going with me for support.

They ask me, mommy, mommy. You know, they're preparing me, they're preparing.

I said, I don't know. I'm like stone. Sometimes I feel I am stone. Inside, you know.

**UNITED
STATES
HOLOCAUST
MEMORIAL
MUSEUM**

Dedication Ceremony

*Thursday,
April 22, 1993*

*Seating begins
at 8:30 a.m.*

*All guests must be
seated by 10:30 a.m.*

*Ceremony begins
at 11:00 a.m.*

*100 Raoul Wallenberg
Place, SW (at 15th Street
and Independence Avenue)*

*Take Metro subway on
the orange or blue line to
Smithsonian, exit on
Independence Avenue, walk
two blocks west to Museum*

Admit One to Section C

*This ticket is
non-transferable*

April 23, 1993
Washington DC

ALINA: You know, the museum is just built right. Stones and metal. Right, Jared? You weren't there, but that's what we saw. Stones and iron.

March 18, 1994
Tamarac

ALINA: Yad Vashem is like, a light is burning always there. You were there?

JARED: No. I haven't been there.

ALINA: It's like a memorial. You put a stone, like somebody dies from the family. Like my husband, he has a stone. And you put names on it, and there are names of all the camps, and the light . . .

But this in Washington is like real concentration camp. And you walk in and get chills up your spine. Like you remember, but you don't know from where, because it is different.

March 15, 1994
Tamarac

JARED: So why do you think the museum is important?

ALINA: It's important for people what don't believe. I think that people . . . for me it's important because over there I feel like it's my family. It's my family to remember, you know, in history.

But what I think, if people don't believe, they probably don't want to believe. It's hard to believe the horror and everything. But so many people are alive and a witness to it.

So I figure if another person start to believe it, because this is true story that they are showing there, they're very successful.

April 21, 1993
New Haven
Fortunoff Video Archive at Yale

ALINA: And I'm happy that I now have family. Beautiful children. I lost my husband eight years ago, and I have three beautiful children, and they know that daddy wants them to remember what we went through. They join second generation.

They are very beautiful children, I'm very proud. That's what I have, that's only what I have—my good children and my grandchildren. I have four grandchildren, from one son.

Alina refers here to George's four children, Adam, Lindsay, Kerri, and Allison. After this was recorded Sophia and her husband, Ken Cagan, had two children, Zachary, born May 17, 1994, and Brianna, born December 6, 1996, four months before Alina's death.

Lindsay Bacall, "The Memories of the Nightmare"

April 23, 1993

Alina's granddaughter turned in this essay to her tenth-grade teacher on the opening day of the U.S. Holocaust Memorial Museum. It concerns an earlier visit to a Holocaust memorial in San Francisco.

We drove by a Holocaust memorial. It was a white plaster sculpture standing by a wire fence and looking at the water. I realized that I would not like this stop. It was on the corner of the street and as we made a left turn the bushes covered this disgusting sight. I began to get butterflies in my stomach and they worsened when my stepmother said, "If you didn't like that, you won't like the rest of it." The first thing that came into my mind was: "There is more?"

April 21, 1993
New Haven
Fortunoff Video Archive at Yale

ALINA: I hear that they are showing now in Washington, in the museum, when you walk in, I think part of what we went through. Not everything, but at least a part.

There was a nice article in the newspaper about the shoes. They burn over there everything. Between the shoes, it was my cousin's, my family's, everybody's. You know, the shoes could belong to my family.

April 23, 1993
U.S. Holocaust Memorial Museum
Washington DC

ALINA: Who knows if my mother is not here, the shoes of my parents, my shoes too . . . because they took everything.

Alina reads an inscription on the wall above the pile of shoes from Auschwitz on display at the U.S. Holocaust Memorial Museum.

"We are the shoes, we are the last witnesses. We are shoes from grandchildren and grandfathers, from Prague, Paris, and Amsterdam. And because we are only made of fabric and leather, and not of blood and flesh, each one of us avoided the . . ." What is that? "Hellfire. Hellfire."

That's what I went through . . . but not my shoes, my shoes went probably, too. But this is only from crematorium, Sophie.

April 21, 1993
New Haven
Fortunoff Video Archive at Yale

ALINA: My husband died eight years ago, and I remarried. I have a very good friend now. And funny thing, he's American. He's not from the other side. And I am happy that he listens to me, that he doesn't run away from it. I am talking lately a lot.

DANA: How do you think this is, that now you're talking and not before?

ALINA: I think that's me, I keep a lot in me. And I didn't bring up, and when I start to bring, I start to cry, and I never want to see, anybody to see me crying.

April 23, 1993
Washington DC

ALINA: And that's my sickness. I don't like it when somebody see me crying. Always when I cry, I was hiding.

SOPHIA: When she was sick, I used to get so angry at her, because she wouldn't let me in the room. In the hospital she didn't want anybody to come visit her, and I didn't understand that. I only thought that you would want to be with your children and your family. But she just didn't want anybody to see her hurt or hurting or unhappy or sad.

JARED: Why do you think that is?

ALINA: I don't want to bring pain on others, on my children, on other people that I love. I used to hide a lot of things from my husband about the children, not to hurt him.

SOPHIA: He's just like her, George is just like her. He used to think he could hide it from us, but he can't.

ALINA: Georgie is exactly like me. I don't know if it's good or not, but that's what we are born this way.

January 13, 1985
The Hartford Courant

"Dad, you mustn't get so upset," said George, who is a doctor. "It isn't good for you."

Leo looked at him and continued the story.

April 21, 1993
New Haven
Fortunoff Video Archive at Yale

ALINA: I always was the strong one. I bring the family together, any problems, anything, you know. You raising your kids, you always have problems. And I always want to be strong to help my husband. We worked together.

And I never want to talk. I was very angry at my husband a lot of times, but I was happy he was talking about it because my kids now know a little.

SUSAN: You were angry that he was sharing?

ALINA: Yes, I was afraid because this is terrible stories, murder stories, what you don't want to show your kids on the television, half of it.

Speech delivered by George Bacall at Alina's seventieth birthday party

February 5, 1992

Tamarac

Mom was always a strong, resilient person—the backbone of the family. Yet she was always gentle and caring, always the epitome of the concerned *yidishe mama.*

Mom and Dad finally retired to Florida, where they had a few good years, but Dad's heart condition worsened and we lost him seven years ago.

We all missed him and of course still do—but most hurt was Mom. She had lost her love and her hero.

But Mom understood survival. She was an Olympic champion in survival. She did not give up, and of course, she never burdened her family or friends. Nevertheless, we all understood her loss. You were all there for her and did what you could to ease her pain.

And a few years ago, a handsome, kind, unassuming prince of a man swept her off her feet. Charlie walked into her life.

March 15, 1994

Tamarac

ALINA: He wasn't born in Europe, Charlie.

JARED: I know. You were born in New York.

CHARLIE: Brooklyn. Brooklyn, New York.

JARED: You're an American Jew. You're Jewish, right?

CHARLIE: Yes.

ALINA: He looks like ten Jews, no? He looks like ten Jews.

CHARLIE: You think of a Jew, and you look at me and you see the Jew.

JARED: And you were hearing about what was going on in one form or another, no?

CHARLIE: About the Holocaust?

JARED: About what was going on in Germany and Poland when you . . . do you remember that?

CHARLIE: Not as much as you think, no.

*April 22, 1993.
Courtesy Sophia
Bacall-Cagan.*

JARED: What did you, what did you hear? Do you remember what you knew then or what you didn't know?

CHARLIE: Almost nothing, I'd say. I didn't know about the concentration camps and all that. I don't remember when I actually heard it for the first time that they were gassing the people and . . .

ALINA: Was after war?

CHARLIE: . . . shooting them, you know, lining them up and shooting them.

* * *

ALINA: I call this cemetery. I'm talking to Charlie to go there, when we going to be there. And to see, like once a year to go there.

JARED: How did you feel during the candlelight vigil? That evening after the . . .

ALINA: Yes, I remember. I thought I'm going to light myself, and then I saw somebody light the candle for me. I think I asking you, why it's lit, why I don't light, you know? I want to light the candles. I don't know . . . the little light that is still with me, you know, the little small candle.

And all of them is done and mine is still burning, remember? And mine still was burning, that's . . . you know? And this minute, I don't, I didn't think this is for my parents or for my close family . . . like me, I stayed alive, and this little candle was for me too.

I thinking then about myself. Thank God I stay alive, I have my kids. But I will never dream that I would be alive. In the back of the head here, you know, but it was so hard that you don't believe it.

You want to live, you want to live. But it was so hard to make it. And I stayed alive and have such a beautiful family.

This is the candle. This is my candle with the light, what I brought through, through this war. That's my feeling.

* * *

ALINA: And I'm going back to see the pictures on the wall, you know. I was looking because I sent a lot of pictures from family, I didn't see them.

JARED: You sent them to the museum?

ALINA: Yes. They say they going to make generation pictures, from my mother, father, and . . .

JARED: Did they send them back to you?

ALINA: I have here even my grandmother, you know. They didn't send anything back. They have the pictures.

JARED: The only ones?

ALINA: What?

JARED: Copies?

ALINA: I made copies, yes. I made copies of them. I would not send the real. Maybe they are there, but we didn't have time, too much time . . .

* * *

JARED: After the candlelight vigil, we went into the building, and we went into what they call the Hall of Remembrance, and there was a kind of . . . it became really quiet at one moment, and someone started saying Kaddish. Do you remember that?

ALINA: Yes.

JARED: What did you think?

ALINA: I was stunned. I was only thinking about my mother. I was very close with my mother. And I remember my father, he was, they let him go to camp. My mother they took to crematorium. She was

[123]

a very young woman, beautiful, and I wish, God . . . I was thinking about my mother and my father. That's it, nobody else. Why, I don't know.

JARED: No idea?

ALINA: No.

JARED: And then that night . . .

ALINA: And then, then, yes? That night . . . And I was walking and I didn't feel my kids around, nobody. Just I was, like, in different world. Just I was like a stone, I told you . . . You asked me how I feel. I said, like a stone.

* * *

ALINA: And I'm thinking about it. You know, a lot of people like to talk about it, and I'm always pushing, pushing away, you know, I'm always pushing. I hate to remember, I hate to talk about it, I hate to gripe about it, like I'm pushing away these things. Always I was like that. I talk more now. You know how old I am? When we came to the United States I didn't mention even, nothing. Nobody knows.

JARED: You wanted it to be a secret?

ALINA: I don't know why. I'm thinking about it. I think if I remember even now, you know, when I remember, nothing goes out from my head.

Some things, you know, nothing you can put in book. You can't put any place.